## Have you ever wondered . . .

- How **astrology** got started?
- How **scientific** it actually is?
- Where the names for the **signs of the zodiac** came from?
- What they all **mean**?
- What the real belief behind **reincarnation** is?
- If **prophecy** really is fulfilled?
- What is meant by the **"Age of Aquarius"**?
- About the origin and use of the **Ouija Board**?
- What the ancient Scriptures say about **channeling**?
- How much you can rely on **astrological readings**?

*You'll find the answers in this book!*

# The
# SECRET MESSAGE
## of the
# ZODIAC

## Troy Lawrence

Here's Life Publishers

First Printing, February 1990

Published by
HERE'S LIFE PUBLISHERS, INC.
P. O. Box 1576
San Bernardino, CA 92402

Printed by Dickinson Press, Grand Rapids, MI.
Front cover art: R. DiCianni
Inside illustrations: Bob Bubnis

### Library of Congress Cataloging-in-Publication Data

Lawrence, Troy.
    The secret message of the zodiac / Troy Lawrence.
        p.      cm.
    ISBN 0-89840-280-8
    1. Astrology—Controversial literature.  2. New Age move-
ment—Controversial literature.  3. Occultism—Religious
aspects—Christianity.  4. Christian life—1960-    I. Title.
BF1713.L38   1989
261.5'1—dc20                         89-27768
                                           CIP

Scripture quotations are from the *King James Version.*

### For More Information, Write:

*L.I.F.E.*—P.O. Box A399, Sydney South 2000, Australia
*Campus Crusade for Christ of Canada*—Box 300, Vancouver, B.C., V6C 2X3, Canada
*Campus Crusade for Christ*—Pearl Assurance House, 4 Temple Row, Birmingham, B2 5HG, England
*Lay Institute for Evangelism*—P.O. Box 8786, Auckland 3, New Zealand
*Campus Crusade for Christ*—P.O. Box 240, Raffles City Post Office, Singapore 9117
*Great Commission Movement of Nigeria*—P.O. Box 500, Jos, Plateau State Nigeria, West Africa
*Campus Crusade for Christ International*—Arrowhead Springs, San Bernardino, CA 92414, U.S.A.

# Contents

I. What Is the Aquarian Age? . . . . . . . . 9

II. The Mazzaroth: Signs of the Zodiac . . . 15
    Virgo: The Virgin
    Libra: The Balances
    Scorpio: The Scorpion
    Sagittarius: The Archer
    Capricornus: The Goat-Fish
    Aquarius: The Water-Bearer
    Pisces: The Fishes
    Aries: The Ram (Lamb)
    Taurus: The Ox
    Gemini: The Twins
    Cancer: The Crab (Sheepfold)
    Leo: The Lion

III. Astrology: Science or Superstition? . . . 55
    Astrology Vs. Science
    Astro-Twins
    Astrology Vs. the Bible
    Astrology and Prophecy

IV. Reincarnation: The Wheel of Rebirth . . 71
    Reincarnation Vs. History
    Reincarnation Vs. the Bible

V. Channeling: Is It From God? . . . . . . 85
    The Ouija Board
    Channeling and Christ
    Channeling Vs. the Bible

VI. Prophecy: True or False? . . . . . . . . 95
    Jeane Dixon's Prophecies
    Bible Prophecies and Their Fulfillment
    Daniel's Timetable

VII. Choose You This Day . . . . . . . . 117
    Notes . . . . . . . . . . . . . . . . . 122
    Bibliography . . . . . . . . . . . . . . 125

# THE TWELVE SIGNS OF THE ZODIAC

# AND THEIR DECANS

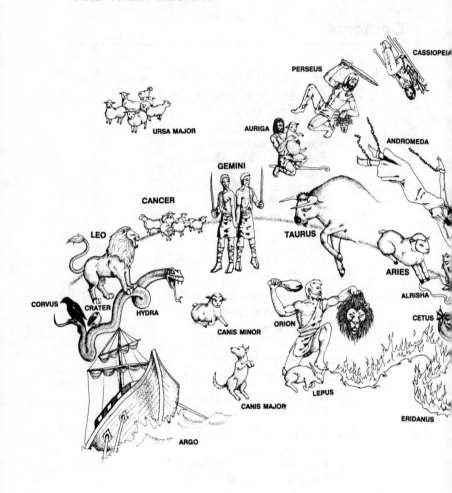

| LEO | GEMINI | ARIES |
|---|---|---|
| HYDRA | LEPUS | CASSIOPEIA |
| CRATER | CANIS MAJOR | CETUS |
| CORVUS | CANIS MINOR | PERSEUS |
| | | |
| CANCER | TAURUS | PISCES |
| URSA MAJOR | ORION | ALRISHA |
| URSA MINOR | ERIDANUS | ANDROMEDA |
| ARGO | AURIGA | CEPHEUS |

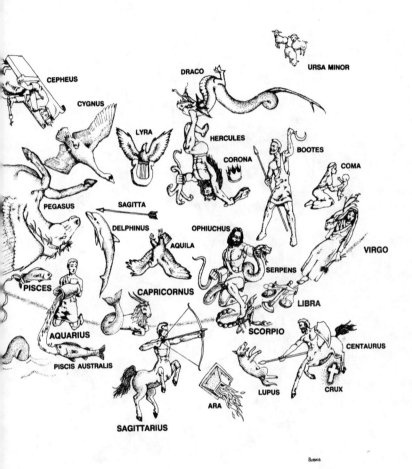

CEPHEUS

DRACO

URSA MINOR

CYGNUS

LYRA

HERCULES

BOOTES

CORONA

COMA

PEGASUS

SAGITTA

DELPHINUS

OPHIUCHUS

AQUILA

VIRGO

SERPENS

PISCES

CAPRICORNUS

LIBRA

AQUARIUS

SCORPIO

CENTAURUS

PISCIS AUSTRALIS

LUPUS

CRUX

ARA

SAGITTARIUS

Burkis

**AQUARIUS**
  PISCIS AUSTRALIS
  PEGASUS
  CYGNUS

**SAGITTARIUS**
  LYRA
  ARA
  DRACO

**LIBRA**
  CRUX
  LUPUS
  CORONA

**CAPRICORNUS**
  SAGITTA
  AQUILA
  DELPHINUS

**SCORPIO**
  SERPENS
  OPHIUCHUS
  HERCULES

**VIRGO**
  COMA
  BOOTES
  CENTAURUS

BUBNIS

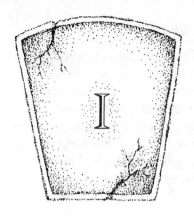

# What Is the Aquarian Age?

The so-called Piscean and Aquarian Ages are related to certain astronomical facts, particularly the *precession of the equinoxes*. The *equinoxes* are the two days of the year when the sun is directly above the equator. One of the days, in March, is called the "vernal equinox." The other, the "autumnal equinox," occurs in September. As the earth orbits the sun, the position of the sun changes in relation to the earth. The sun appears north of the equator between the March and September equinoxes, and south of the equator between the September and March equinoxes. We will discuss the precession of these equinoxes later. The influences this precession of the equinoxes are said to have upon human affairs are associated with the doctrines of *astrology*.

According to history, the Babylonians and the Chaldeans were among the first to chart the heavens. The early shepherds in what was known as Mesopotamia gazed at the inky canopy of those heavens and were fascinated by the myriad points of light which seemed to descend so low they could be touched. Night after night, century after century, those people watched and meditated upon the celestial phenomena. Eventually, they were able to record the movements of certain planets as well as theorize regarding their nature.

The *ecliptic,* or path of the sun on its celestial journey, is known as the *zodiac.* The ancients ascribed to this course of the sun in the heavens twelve figures through which the moon passed each month and the sun once a year. Along this path, too, they noted the passage of the five planets visible to the naked eye. According to the theory of the Babylonians, which became the foundation of astrology, the heavenly bodies have a correspondence or sympathetic relationship with the earth and all things of worldly existence.

The rulers of the zodiac were gods; that is, the celestial bodies were thought of as being divine intelligences. These rulers were Sin, Shamash and Ishtar, or the Moon, the Sun and Venus. The moving planets served as interpreters of the divine will, while the fixed stars were agents or modifiers of such will. The position of the moving body relative to a stationary one suggested a specific meaning. These meanings were transferred to corresponding earthly powers and to man's own nature. As a result, the destiny of man and his welfare were said to be subject to these celestial manifestations of the divine will.

The word *zodiac* is derived from the Greek root word meaning "life." It is significant, too, that *zoion* is the Greek diminutive for *zoon*, meaning "animal," because some of the symbolical divisions of the zodiac, as well as some other stars, have been made to resemble animals. The Hebrew name for zodiac was *mazzaroth* which means "encircle" or "surround" which the ecliptic (or path of the sun) appears to do. The Chaldean word for zodiac was *mizrata* (watches). The early astrologers, who were elementary astronomers, were called *watchers* of the stars. The Chaldeans saw the position of the stars as alluding to a council of the conceived divine beings to determine the effects that were to be had upon human beings, elements and events. Their phrase for this group was "Divinities of the Council."

The zodiacal signs are actually twelve constellations or star groups. Some have said these constellations "girdle the earth in the path of the Sun." The term *sign* comes from their symbolic form. These are Aries, Taurus, Gemini, Cancer, Leo, Virgo, Libra, Scorpio, Sagittarius, Capricorn, Aquarius, and Pisces. The ancient shepherds and herdsmen gazed long at the star groups and imagined their form to resemble earthly objects. Thus there appeared to the ancients to be a water-bearer, an ox, a pair of fish, balances, and other common objects. This visual suggestion is similar to the images various cloud formations seem to us to assume today. The zodiacal signs or constellations also indicate the twelve divisions of the ecliptic, thirty degrees each. In fact, astronomically, the zodiac itself refers to the constellations of the ecliptic.

The course of the great stars gives the divisions of the calendar, the day, year, world year, and world era. A new world era begins whenever the sun on the day of the spring, or vernal, equinox enters a new sign of the zodiac. According to this theory, the position of the sun on the vernal equinox moves eastward from year to year. In 72 years it moves one day, and in about 2200 years, one month – or into a new sign. The period of the 2200 years, therefore, is the world era or what is astrologically referred to as an "age," according to which of the signs the equinox occurs in, such as Aries, Pisces or Aquarius. This changing position of the sun on the vernal equinox is called the "precession of the equinoxes."

To understand the astronomical hypothesis of what this precession is and how it occurs, imagine a spinning top. The axis of the top is an imaginary vertical line through its center from bottom to top. If we disturb the top, it continues to spin, but its axis precesses, or moves, around the vertical center, tracing out a cone. The axis deviates from its vertical position, gradually moving in a circle or a cone around it. The earth's axis also describes a cone, or one complete revolution, in a cycle of nearly 26,000 years.

The cause of the precession is the attraction of the sun and the moon to the equatorial protuberance or *bulge* of the earth. The angle of the axis of the earth, in relationship to the sun and the moon, causes the earth to expose the larger bulk of its matter along the equator to the sun and the moon. These bodies, the sun and moon, tend to align the equator on the same plane as the ecliptic, that is, cause the earth's equator and the ecliptic or sun's path to be parallel with each other. Though this is not accomplished perfectly, it does account for the axis of the earth gradually changing over a period of 26,000 years and tracing a cone as explained.

As a consequence of this precession, the star toward which the North Pole points, the polestar, changes with each revolution of the axis. Today the North Pole points to Polaris. In 3000 B.C., when Egypt's Great Pyramid was being built, the North Star was Draconis. At that time, the vernal equinox occurred in the zodiacal sign of Aries.

However, because the earth's axis gradually revolves, it appears, as we look toward the heavens, that the zodiacal signs or constellations are moving westward. This, with the sun's position seeming to move eastward as we said above, results in the vernal equinox eventually taking place under a new sign, which brings about a new *world era* or *age*. The beginning of spring no longer occurs in the sign of Aries — it has been in Pisces for some time. In fact, it is believed astronomically that we have now even left the Piscean Age and entered the Aquarian Age, or that we will within a very few years.

Each of these ages is said to have a cosmic, a physical and a psychological influence upon the earth and on man corresponding to the symbol representing it. To the ancients the stars composing the constellation *Pisces* resembled two fish, tied by the tail with a long ribbon. It is called a "water" sign. There are various theories as to how water became identified with the sign, aside from the purely psychological one of similarity. It is pointed out that at the beginning of the Piscean Age Christ chose fishermen as His disciples, and that baptism played a prominent part in early Christian rites. The fish miracles of the Bible are seen related to the Piscean Age. Also, there is reference to the great sea conquests of the last twenty centuries and the development of steam as a source of power.

The next age into which we advance by the precession of equinoxes, as we have said, is the *Aquarian*. The water-bearer pouring water into the mouth of a writhing fish is the age-old symbol for this sign. Along with the New Age will come, many say, a New Age Messiah. As Jesus was the Messiah of the Piscean Age, there will come a like figure for the new Aquarian Age. His purpose? To lead mankind into the next stage of cosmic evolution.

Through the years I studied astrology, I was always curious about the signs themselves. Notwithstanding the effect they had, purportedly, on our lives, I wanted to know what they actually meant. Discovering this would not be easy.

No astrologist, famous or unknown, could tell me anything. They could tell me all about how the signs affect one another, the houses, decans, relationships to other constellations, etc., but the actual *signs* were a complete mystery among the entire international astrological community. In fact, one of them told me, "Don't worry about what they might mean — whatever they meant has long been lost — let's just worry about how they affect us!"

I was not satisfied, though. I had to discover why these particular signs were chosen for certain star groups. What was their esoteric meaning? What is the meaning of the water-bearer? What is the message of Capricorn, the head and torso of a dying goat with back parts of a writhing fish? What is the meaning of the scales (Libra), the ox (Taurus), and all the other creatures and objects?

I was certain that if I uncovered the secret message of the zodiac, I would find marvelous hidden treasures, for example, possibly the identity of the Christ or Messiah of the Aquarian Age. The signs were there for a purpose, and I wanted to discover what that purpose was.

I started my quest by comparing various astrological charts and found that other cultures do not always use the same signs we use. The Chinese, for example, use such things as a horse, dog, chicken, etc. The ancient Chinese signs had been the same as our occidental version, but a long time ago, a Chinese emperor had changed them.

I also discovered, surprisingly, that the earliest charts of the zodiac were Hebrew. The Greeks derived their knowledge of the zodiac from the Hebrews; the Romans got their information from the Arabs, who also had received it from the Hebrews. So I had to look to the record of the Hebrews, the Bible, to solve the mystery. That much-misunderstood text had been recorded by gifted seers thousands of years ago — about the same time the Hebrew zodiac came into being.

If I could uncover the hidden meaning of these signs, I could unveil the great truths originally declared by those who created the signs. Little did I know that I was about to embark on an awesome tour. I would indeed discover long-hidden secrets, shrouded information that nonetheless left a clear message for our time!

With that, let us press on. Ponder carefully as we unravel ancient mysteries, and decode the secret message of the zodiac.

# II

# The Mazzaroth: Signs of the Zodiac

The psalmist has written that even the stars in their constellations declare the glory of God:

> The heavens declare the glory of God; and the firmament sheweth His handywork. Day unto day uttereth speech, and night unto night sheweth knowledge. There is no speech nor language, where their voice is not heard (Psalm 19:1-3).

What is this knowledge and wisdom of God that is revealed through the constellations? We read further that God created the heavens, and they were to be given for *signs* to the inhabitants of the earth:

> And God said, Let there be lights in the firmament of the heaven to divide the day from the night; and let them be for signs, and for seasons, and for days, and years (Genesis 1:14).

In other verses in the Bible we read that the constellations indeed bear a message:

> The heavens declare his righteousness, and all the people see his glory (Psalm 97:6).

> Lift up your eyes on high, and behold who hath created these things, that bringeth out their host by number: he calleth them all by names by the greatness of His might, for that he is strong in power; not one faileth (Isaiah 40:26).

**15**

He telleth the number of the stars; he calleth them all by their names (Psalm 147:4).

Seek him that maketh the seven stars and Orion, and turneth the shadow of death into the morning, and maketh the day dark with night: that calleth for the waters of the sea, and poureth them out upon the face of the earth: The LORD is his name (Amos 5:8).

Canst thou bind the sweet influences of Pleiades, or loose the bands of Orion? Canst thou bring forth Mazzaroth in his season? or canst thou guide Arcturus with his sons? Knowest thou the ordinances of heaven? canst thou set the dominion thereof in the earth? (Job 38:31-33)

*Mazzaroth* means the signs of the zodiac, and Orion, Arcturus, and Pleides are several of these signs. The Bible says that the heavens not only show the splendor of a creator, but are given as signs to those who dwell upon the earth. The prophets declare that the constellations were given as signs, and that the Lord has numbered and named the stars.

In my quest to decode the secret message of the zodiac, I found that the Bible itself speaks of the "ordinances" of heaven. The signs of the zodiac can be found in every nation of the earth, like a universal language. This universal language of the stars contains a very important message long since lost in obscurity. In this booklet, we shall discover what this message is.

The Mazzaroth (zodiac) is divided into twelve constellations; each of these constellations has a sign and three sub-signs. The sub-signs are called *decans*. Among the ancients of all nations the constellations were given figures of men, women, animals and things as signs, varying only a little from nation to nation and from age to age. These signs are:

I.   *Virgo: The Virgin.* The figure is a young woman with an ear of wheat in one hand and a branch in the other.

II. *Libra: The Balances.* The figure is a pair of balances in the act of weighing.

III. *Scorpio: The Scorpion.* The figure is a deadly scorpion poised to strike.

IV. *Sagittarius: The Archer.* The figure is a horse with the torso, head and arms of a man, holding a drawn bow, ready to shoot.

V. *Capricornus: The Goat-Fish.* The figure is a dying goat with the tail of a withering fish.

VI. *Aquarius: The Water-Bearer.* The figure is a man with a large urn which is pouring forth a stream of water.

VII. *Pisces: The Fishes.* The figure is two large fish, connected by a long band, one end of which is tied to the tail of one fish, and the other end tied to the tail of the other fish. One fish swims toward the North Star.

VIII. *Aries: The Ram.* The figure is a strong ram.

IX. *Taurus: The Ox.* The figure is a powerful ox pushing forward.

X. *Gemini: The Twins.* The figure is two young men.

XI. *Cancer: The Crab.* The figure is a crab, but originally this sign was a sheepfold.

XII. *Leo: The Lion.* The figure is a great lion with his feet on top of and crushing a crooked serpent.

These twelve signs do not stand alone, but each of them has three decans (parts) associated with them. They are:

I. The Decans of Virgo
Coma: the Infant, the Branch, the Desired One
Centaurus: the Despised One
Bootes: the Coming One, the Shepherd

II. The Decans of Libra
Crux: the Cross
Lupus: the Victim
Corona: the Crown

III. The Decans of Scorpio
Serpens: the Serpent
Ophiuchus: the Serpent Holder
Hercules: the Mighty One

IV. The Decans of Sagittarius
Lyra: the Harp
Ara: the Altar
Draco: the Dragon

V. The Decans of Capricornus
Sagitta: the Arrow
Aquila: the Eagle
Delphinus: the Dolphin

VI. The Decans of Aquarius
Piscis Australis: the Southern Fish
Pegasus: the Winged Horse
Cygnus: the Swan

VII. The Decans of Pisces
Alrisha: the Band
Andromeda: the Chained Woman
Cepheus: the Crowned King

VIII. The Decans of Aries
Cassiopeia: the Enthroned Woman
Cetus: the Sea-Monster
Perseus: the Breaker

IX. The Decans of Taurus
Orion: the Dayspring

Eridanus: the River of the Judge
Auriga: the Shepherd

X. The Decans of Gemini
Lepus: the Hare
Canis Major: the Great Dog
Canis Minor: the Lesser Dog

XI. The Decans of Cancer
Ursa Major: the Greater Sheepfold
Ursa Minor: the Lesser Sheepfold
Argo: the Ship

XII. The Decans of Leo
Hydra: the Serpent
Crater: the Bowl or Cup of Wrath
Corvus: the Raven

## The Signs

These particular signs were given for a reason, but the purpose and message has been lost to astrology. Let us discover their hidden meanings.

# Virgo:
# The Virgin

The Virgin, one of the largest constellations, lies about half north and half south of the equator and south of Coma and Bootes. The sun occupies Virgo for forty-three days, passing through it from September 14th to October 29th. Since most of its stars are comparatively faint, and much scattered, it is difficult to trace. Virgo is represented by a woman with a branch in her right hand and a cluster of seeds in her left. In Hebrew she is called Bethulah (virgin). Thus is pictured the fulfillment of Isaiah 7:14 as quoted by Matthew:

> Behold, a virgin shall be with child, and shall bring forth a son, and they shall call his name Emmanuel, which being interpreted is, God with us (Matthew 1:23).

The star at her right hand is called Spica, the branch. The Hebrews call it Tsemech (the branch). The Lord spoke of His Christ to the ancients through Zechariah the prophet. He said:

> For behold, I will bring forth my servant the BRANCH (Zechariah 3:8).

One of the stars in the arm carrying the branch is called Al Mureddin, which means he who shall have dominion. Psalm 72:8 states:

> He shall have dominion also from sea to sea.

Another star near the head is called Zavijava (gloriously beautiful), and is the exact same word used in Isaiah

4:2 regarding the Branch of Jehovah:

> In that day shall the Branch of the LORD be beautiful
> and glorious.

In her left hand she holds a cluster of seeds. This
reminds us that Christ is the "seed of the woman" who
shall bruise the serpent's head (Genesis 3:15). According
to the Bible, one of the descendants of the woman (Eve)
would overcome the adversary (Satan). The Bible claims
that Jesus has done this by His death on the cross. Satan
brought death and sin into the world, but Jesus has
brought life and salvation.

COMA (the Desired). The first decan of Virgo is a
woman with a child in her arms. The meaning of the name
of this decan, the desired, is the identical word used by
Haggai when he prophesied of the coming Messiah:

> The desire of all nations shall come (2:7).

It is said that the Star of Bethlehem appeared in
this constellation. The Magi (wise men) were told by a
prophet of Persia that God Himself would be born of a
virgin among the Jews, and that the sign of the birth
would be a new star in a certain constellation. That
prophet was Zoroaster, and many of his followers can still
be found today in Iran (Persia) and India. The Buddhists
wait for the coming of Maitreya: the Merciful One. Gua-
tama Sidhartha, the sage of India, said that one would
come who would be greater than a thousand Buddhas.

The disciples of Buddha came to him and asked,
"Master, how will we know Him when He appears?"

Gautama replied, "He shall be known as Maitreya."

He was to come forth in the "Western Paradise." In
the Bible Jesus is called the Son of God (Mark 1:1), and
His Father is called the Father of mercies (2 Corinthians
1:3). Jesus is Lord, and, "The LORD is merciful" (Psalm

103:8). To the west of India, in a land called Israel, the Merciful One was born of a virgin. The Hindus still wait for Kalki, the last avatar (incarnation) of Vishnu. He will, they say, conquer and slay the wicked. They do not know when he is to come, but they picture him riding a white horse and carrying a double-edged sword in his mouth. This reminds me of how Jesus' second coming is described in the Bible:

> And I saw heaven opened, and behold a white horse; and he that sat upon him was called Faithful and True, and in righteousness he doth judge and make war . . . and his name is called The Word of God . . . And out of his mouth goeth a sharp sword (Revelation 19:11-15).

In my studies of the religions of the ancient world, I learned that all the nations expected the coming of the one who would redeem them. For example, once a year at the appropriate time, the Scandinavians would sacrifice a man upon a tree. They would thrust a spear into his side and call his name Balder (savior). The Egyptians looked toward Osiris, one who would die and be resurrected from the dead. The Aztecs longed for Quetzalcoatl, the winged serpent who would die, descend into Hades, and rise again. The ancient Chinese longed for Tien, the Son of Heaven.

Yet none of these figures were ever real! They were just myths. The only savior-god we have a history of is Jesus of Nazareth. Could it be that He is the one the nations have longed for? Could it be that He, and He alone, is the "desire of all nations"?

CENTAURUS (the Despised). In both Hebrew and Arabic the meaning of this sign is the despised. The coming Savior is called by the prophet Isaiah:

> He is despised and rejected of men; a man of sorrows, and acquainted with grief: and we hid as it were our faces from him; he was despised, and we esteemed him not (Isaiah 53:3).

Yet He laid down His own life. This is shown by the spear in the hand of the centaur, piercing the heart of the victim, represented by the decan Lupus (the slain one). Jesus said:

> I lay down my life that I might take it again. No man taketh it from me, but I lay it down of myself. I have power to lay it down, and I have power to take it again (John 10:17,18).

The chief star in this decan is Alpha Centauri. The Hebrews called it Toliman: the heretofore and the hereafter. Jesus is called this in Revelation 1:8.

The Greek name for this decan was Cheiron: the pierced. There was a fable in ancient Greece about a certain man named Cheiron. He was renowned for his wisdom and prophecy, but was despised because he was a centaur: He had the head and torso of a man, but the body of a horse. Although immortal and despised, he voluntarily died in the place of another for whom a poisoned arrow was intended.

Could this be a corruption of an even more ancient truth? According to the Bible the Messiah would ride into Jerusalem upon a donkey (Zechariah 9:9), but would be rejected and despised (Isaiah 53:3). He would be pierced in His hands and feet (Psalm 22:16). Jesus entered Jerusalem riding upon a colt, and He was rejected and despised. He was lifted up upon a cross and crucified. His hands and feet were pierced by nails, and a spear thrust through His side.

In the zodiac, Centaurus practically surrounds the decan Crux: the cross.

BOOTES (the Coming One). This is the final decan accompanying Virgo. This sign depicts a man with a spear in his right hand and a sickle in his left. The names of the stars in this decan carry a wealth of meaning. Arcturus

(Job 9:9) is a bright star in his knee and means He cometh. Al Katurops in the spear-head means treading under foot. Isaiah refers to the coming Christ:

> I will tread them in mine anger ... For the day of vengeance is in mine heart, and the year of my redeemed is come (Isaiah 63:3,4).

The star in his head, Nekka, means the pierced (Zechariah 12:10).

Bootes is depicted with a sickle in his hand, and is represented as a reaper. In a vision, John so beholds Him:

> And I looked, and behold a white cloud, and upon the cloud one sat like unto the Son of man, having on his head a golden crown and in his hand a sharp sickle. And another angel came out of the temple, crying with a loud voice to him that sat on the cloud, Thrust in thy sickle, and reap: for the time is come for thee to reap; for the harvest of the earth is ripe. And he that sat on the cloud thrust in his sickle on the earth; and the earth was reaped (Revelation 14:14-16).

The constellation of Virgo tells the story of a virgin who shall conceive and bear a son. This son is the branch and seed of the woman, and He will bruise the head of the serpent. He is the desired one of all nations. He is despised of men, but He sacrifices Himself for them. He is coming again as a reaper, to trample and burn the lost but to harvest the redeemed.

# Libra:
# The Balances

The Balances, or scales, convey the idea of purchase, and Jesus came to buy or redeem us from death and Hell. The name of this constellation, with its three decans, gives the complete picture of this redemption.

In Hebrew its name is Mozanaim (the scales, weighing) but in Arabic the name is Al Zubena, signifying purchase or redemption. In Coptic it is Lambadia, meaning station of propitiation.

Libra contains three bright stars, the brightest of which is named Zuben El Genubi, meaning the purchase, or price which is deficient. It signifies weighed in the balances and found wanting. However, while man is thus found wanting, Zuben El Shemali, a bright star in the upper scale, means the price which covers. This star has another name, Al Gubi, meaning heaped up or high, giving the infinite value of the price of redemption. A third star in this constellation below and toward Centaurus and the victim slain is called Zuben Akrabi, meaning the price of the conflict.

God revealed Himself in the Lord Jesus. Isaiah says of the Messiah:

> Who hath measured the waters in the hollow of his hand, and meted out heaven with the span, and comprehended the dust of the earth in a measure, and weighed the mountains in scales, and the hills in a balance? (Isaiah 40:12)

The Messiah is not only the Redeemer, but He is the Creator of this creation as well!

Libra foreshadows the sacrifice of Christ for the purpose of redeeming His people and bringing salvation to all mankind. Further detail is given in the accompanying decans of the cross endured, the victim slain, and the crown bestowed.

CRUX (the Cross). The Hebrew name of this constellation is Adom, which means cutting off. Daniel refers to the fact that "after threescore and two weeks shall Messiah be cut off" (Daniel 9:26).

At the time of the coming of Jesus Christ this Southern Cross was visible in the latitude of Jerusalem. Since the time when the real sacrifice was offered at Jerusalem, and through the gradual recession of the Polar Star, it has become invisible there.

According to the Bible, Jesus was the Messiah who was cut off (upon the cross) to redeem fallen mankind.

LUPUS (the Victim). In the ancient zodiac the original sign of this decan of Libra was not a wolf, but a lion. He was pictured as dying or dead, with his tongue sticking out of his mouth, as if thirsty. Is this not the Lion of the Tribe of Judah? He came to death saying:

> I am poured out like water . . . my strength is dried up (Psalm 22:14,15).

When Jesus said, "I thirst" (John 19:28), He was given vinegar to drink.

The Romans changed the sign to a wolf because the wolf, which they hunted, was a much more familiar beast to them. Yet, the original sign was a lion. Jesus, the Lion of Judah, offered Himself up in death as a victim to atone for the sins of mankind.

CORONA (the Crown). In Hebrew the name of this

constellation is Atarah, meaning a royal crown. Its stars are known today in the East by the plural Ataroth.

Thus the cross is closely followed by the crown and reminds us of the statement in Revelation regarding the triumph of Jesus Christ:

> Thou art worthy . . . for thou wast slain, and hast re-deemed us to God by thy blood (Revelation 5:9).

Paul says in Hebrews that God has crowned Jesus with "glory and honour" (Hebrews 2:9). The world put a crown of thorns upon his head (Matthew 27:29), but He has received also a "crown of life" (James 1:12). Those who follow Jesus will receive crowns as well and "they shall be as the stones of a crown" (Zechariah 9:16).

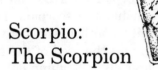

## Scorpio: The Scorpion

In Hebrew the name of this constellation is Akrab, which is the name of a scorpion. It also can mean conflict, war or enmity. The star picture is a scorpion endeavoring to sting the heel of a mighty man who is struggling with a serpent. The scorpion is being crushed by the man who has his foot placed on its heart.

The scorpion is a deadly enemy and all the names associated with this constellation set forth the malignant enmity between the serpent and the woman's seed (Genesis 3:15). The Bible gives the history of that enmity in the attempts to destroy all the males of the seed of Abraham (Exodus 1), in the efforts of Athaliah to destroy "all the seed royal" (2 Kings 11), and in the inciting of Herod to destroy all the babes of Bethlehem (Matthew 2).

The enemy struck and the seed was wounded unto death at the cross, but He rose from the grave beyond the power of men or devils ever to interfere with Him.

Jesus is known as the seed of the woman. After Eve had partaken of the forbidden fruit,

> The LORD God said unto the woman, What is this that thou hast done? And the woman said, The serpent beguiled me, and I did eat. And the LORD God said unto the serpent, Because thou hast done this, thou art cursed above all cattle, and above every beast of the field; upon thy belly shalt thou go, and dust shalt thou eat all the days of thy life: And I will put enmity between thee and the woman, and between thy seed and her seed; it shall bruise thy head, and thou shalt bruise his heel (Genesis 3:13-16).

In the ancient world scorpions were known as the seed of the serpent. As the scorpion tries to strike the heel of Ophiuchus, the man crushes the scorpion. Here we have the picture of the enmity (conflict, war) between the seed of the woman (Jesus) and the seed of the serpent. When Jesus returns, He literally will stamp out all conflict and war, and peace shall reign over the earth.

HERCULES (the Mighty Man). He is a man kneeling on one knee, humbled in the conflict, but holding aloft the tokens of victory. His foot is on the head of the dragon. In his right hand he wields a club and in his left he grasps the triple-headed monster, Cerberus. He has the skin of a lion, which he has slain, thrown around him.

The brightest star in his head is named Ras Al Gethi, and means the head of him who bruises. Other stars are Kornephorus, meaning the kneeling branch, Marsic the wounded, Ma'asyn the sin-offering, and Caiam the punished.

Who is the real Hercules? Of Him it is written:

> Thou shalt tread upon the lion and adder: the young lion and the dragon shalt thou trample under feet (Psalm 91:13).

Jesus is the Mighty Man, mighty because He is the Almighty incarnated. It is He who is bruised for our iniquities. It is He who is the Branch. It is He who is wounded for our transgressions (Isaiah 53). It is He who, as the Lion of Judah, offered Himself up as a final offering for sin.

## Sagittarius: The Archer

In Hebrew and Syriac the name of this constellation is Kesith, which means the archer. The Arabic name is Al Kaus, meaning the arrow. Here we have the picture of the centaur as to his outward form: a being with two natures. According to ancient Greek fables, this Sagittarius is Cheiron, the chief centaur who is noble in character, righteous in his dealings, and divine in his power. He is shown coming forth like an arrow from the bow, "full of grace," but as a conqueror. He aims his arrow at the scorpion.

The Hebrew names of the brightest stars are significant: Naim, which means the gracious one, and Nehushta meaning the going and the sending forth.

Bible students can readily identify all this as a prophecy of Him who is to come forth possessing all power and wisdom, conquering His enemies.

John writes of the return of Jesus:

> I saw . . . a white horse: and he that sat on him had a
> bow . . . and he went forth conquering, and to conquer
> (Revelation 6:2).

The Bible also tells us that the Lord slays His enemies with His bow:

> Thine arrows are sharp in the heart of the king's ene-
> mies; whereby the people fall under thee. Thy throne,
> O God, is for ever and ever: the sceptre of thy kingdom
> is a right sceptre (Psalm 45:5,6).

Who are the enemies that Jesus shall conquer? They are represented by the scorpion: war and conflict.

LYRA (the Harp). With the coming forth of the conqueror, this constellation prefigures the praise prepared for him. The brightest star in this sign is one of the most glorious in the heavens and is called Vega, which means He shall be exalted. We read in the Revelation:

> And after these things I heard a great voice of much
> people in heaven saying, Alleluia; Salvation, and glory,
> and honour, and power, unto the Lord our God: For
> true and righteous are his judgments (Revelation
> 19:1,2).

In the zodiac, Lyra is pictured as an eagle carrying the harp upward. We are told in the Bible to

> praise the LORD with harp: sing unto him with the psal-
> tery and an instrument of ten strings (Psalm 33:2).

The Bible also likens the servants of God to eagles. The Lord said Israel would "fly as an eagle" and "spread his wings over Moab" (Jeremiah 48:40). Isaiah says those who "wait upon the LORD shall renew their strength; they shall mount up with wings as eagles" (Isaiah 40:31). The picture of Lyra is of the prayers and singing of the saints ascending up to heaven on the wings of eagles.

ARA (the Altar). An altar or burning pyre is placed upside down with its burning fires pointing downward toward the lower region, which is called Tartarus, meaning the abyss or outer darkness.

Here we have a sign of the judgment of God to befall the wicked:

> Thou shalt make them as a fiery oven in the time of thine anger: the LORD shall swallow them up in his wrath, and the fire shall devour them (Psalm 21:9).

Jesus refers to the outer darkness into which men are to be cast for failure to comply with the conditions imposed upon the guests invited to the marriage supper (Matthew 22:13).

DRACO (the Dragon). This constellation foreshadows the final destruction of the devil and all his works, he who has deceived all the world. It is against him that the God-Man, Jesus, goes forth to war. In the Greek the name of this decan means trodden on. The Bible says:

> The dragon shalt thou trample under feet (Psalm 91:13).

The brightest star is named Thuban, which in the Hebrew means the subtle. Rastaban, a star in the head, means the head of the subtle. The next star in the head is called Ethanin, which means the dragon.

The picture in the heavens represents the dragon twisted and writhing as if being cast out. We read in Revelation 12:9 that the dragon was cast out from heaven.

Thus, the combined testimony of this constellation is the conqueror who shall return with judgment upon the wicked, the one who had Satan and his angels cast out, the one whom the saints praise with song and harp.

# Capricornus:
# The Goat-Fish

In the heavens we have the sign of the head and torso of a dying goat, while the tail is a living fish. What could be the meaning of this strange sign? Let's see.

The Lord spoke unto His people Israel saying, "Take ye a kid of the goats for a sin offering" (Leviticus 9:3). So Aaron "took the goat, which was the sin offering for the people, and slew it, and offered it for sin" (Leviticus 9:15). Moses said of the sacrificial goat that "it is most holy, and God hath given it to you to bear the iniquity of the congregation, to make atonement for them before the LORD" (Leviticus 10:17). Isaiah prophesied that the Messiah would bear our iniquities:

> Surely he hath borne our griefs, and carried our sorrows: yet we did esteem him stricken, smitten of God, and afflicted. But he was wounded for our transgressions, he was bruised for our iniquities: the chastisement of our peace was upon him; and with his stripes we are healed (Isaiah 53:4,5).

Because of sin, which means wrongdoing, we work up a spiritual debt that can be paid back only by suffering. Jesus came to suffer in our place and to pay that debt, or redeem us, so that we may be free of death and hell.

The sign of the goat dying symbolizes the sacrifice of the Son of God, for He was the sacrificial goat. Yet, what does the writhing fishtail mean? When Jacob blessed his sons he promised that they would become a great multitude. Balaam, a prophet from the East who apparently

was inspired of God before his fall, said the seed of Jacob
(Israel) would be in many waters (Numbers 24:7), like
fish. The Lord Himself likened His people to a multitude
of fish. His prophets were to act as fishermen to gather
them to Him (Jeremiah 16:16). Amos said:

> The Lord GOD hath sworn by his holiness that, lo, the
> days shall come upon you, that he will take you away
> with hooks, and your posterity with fishhooks (Amos
> 4:2).

The people of God were likened unto fishes, and it
is through the sacrifice of the Sin Offering that we shall
be made alive! This explains the sign of the dying goat and
the living fish: Capricorn.

SAGITTA (the Arrow). The afflictions that the
Lord brings to the wicked, or to those who need the chastisement of a loving Father, are called His arrows. Job
cries out,

> For the arrows of the Almighty are within me, the
> poison whereof drinketh up my spirit: the terrors of
> God do set themselves in array against me (Job 6:4).

David, stricken by the Lord because of his iniquities, cries,

> O LORD, rebuke me not in thy wrath: neither chasten
> me in thy hot displeasure. For thine arrows stick fast
> in me, and thy hand presseth me sore (Psalm 38:1,2).

Balaam prophesied that the Christ, called from
Egypt, would confound His enemies:

> God brought him forth out of Egypt; he hath as it were
> the strength of an unicorn: he shall eat up the nations
> of his enemies, and shall break their bones, and pierce
> them through with his arrows (Numbers 24:8).

AQUILA (the Eagle). Here we have a picture of the
effect of the arrow in the pierced, fallen, and wounded
eagle. The names of the stars in this decan mean the

wounded, the pierced, and wounded in the heel. We see that the Lord Himself was pierced and wounded for our sins. We have already seen how the Lord is represented as an eagle.

DELPHINUS (the Dolphin). The sign is that of a dolphin rising swiftly out of the sea. To the ancients death was likened to going under the sea:

> Deep calleth unto deep at the noise of thy waterspouts: all thy waves and thy billows are gone over me (Psalm 42:7).

Death is called the sea, and at the last day men shall rise out of it into the resurrection:

> And the sea gave up the dead which were in it; and death and hell delivered up the dead which were in them: and they were judged every man according to their works (Revelation 20:13).

> The Lord said, I will bring again from Bashan, I will bring my people from the depth of the sea (Psalm 68:22).

Paul wrote that in baptism "ye are risen with him through the faith of the operation of God, who hath raised him from the dead" (Colossians 2:12). In baptism we are symbolically buried in death with Christ. Paul said that we bury the old man of sin, and are born again to a newness of life. Just as Jesus was the first to rise from the dead; so His people shall also arise from the dead: like a dolphin jumping forth from the sea.

The constellation of Capricornus tells the story of Jesus as the sacrificial goat who bore our iniquities so that we, the fish, may live. He bore us on eagle's wings, but was smitten by the arrow of God for us. God brought Him out of the depths of death, and He shall bring us from death.

# Aquarius:
# The Water-Bearer

Atonement having been made, the blessings which follow are portrayed in this constellation in the living waters that are poured out for the redeemed. The prophet Balaam prophesied:

> He shall pour the water out of his buckets, and his seed shall be in many waters, and his king shall be higher than Agag, and his kingdom shall be exalted (Numbers 24:7).

The sign in the heavens is a man pouring a stream of water from his bucket. The stream travels downward into the mouth of a dying fish. We already have seen how the fish symbolizes the people of God.

Yet, who was Balaam prophesying of? We read in the New Testament:

> In the last day, that great day of the feast, Jesus stood and cried, saying, If any man thirst, let him come unto me, and drink. He that believeth on me, as the scripture hath said, out of his belly shall flow rivers of living water (John 7:37,38).

Jesus also said:

> Whosoever drinketh of the water that I shall give him shall never thirst; but the water that I shall give him shall be in him a well of water springing up into everlasting life (John 4:14).

The Aquarian Christ is none other than the man of Galilee returned in the glory of the Father. Those who wait for another shall wait in vain.

The star in the right leg of Aquarius is named Scheat, meaning he who returneth.

PISCIS AUSTRALIS (the Southern Fish). We have seen that the people of God are represented as a fish, or fishes. It is Aquarius (Jesus) who restores them to life by His streams of living water. What more can be said of this?

PEGASUS (the Winged Horse). The names of the stars in this decan declare its meaning. The brightest star in the neck of the horse has an ancient Hebrew name, Markab, which means returning from afar. A horse was known for its swiftness, and the Lord has said that He shall return swiftly (Revelation 22:20) with healing in His wings (Malachi 4:2).

CYGNUS (the Swan). In ancient times the swan was known as the bird of return, for it always returned to the place of its birth to give birth. Jesus will come again to Jerusalem. He returns swiftly as a judge of the nations. The brightest star in this decan is called Deneb, the judge.

After the mortal ministry of Jesus, He departed into heaven in a cloud, and two angels stood where He had been and addressed the apostles thus:

> Ye men of Galilee, why stand ye gazing up into heaven? This same Jesus, which is taken up from you into heaven, shall so come in like manner as ye have seen him go up into heaven (Acts 1:11).

The story of the constellation of Aquarius is that of the one prophesied by Balaam: the Messiah of Israel. He shall pour out streams of living waters (His Word) to the people of God (the fish). He shall redeem the fish with His living waters. He shall return swiftly to the place from whence He left.

Jesus Christ is the Great World Teacher who is to come for the Aquarian Age.

## Pisces:
## The Fishes

The Hebrew name of this constellation is Dagim, the fish(es). Balaam prophesied that the seed of Israel would be in many waters, suggesting the idea that they would become a great multitude (see Numbers 24:7), as fish in the seas.

Here we have as the sign in the heavens two identical fish, tied together at each tail with a band, but one swimming toward the North Star. The brightest star is Okda, meaning united. The symbolism is of Judah and Israel. At the time of the Babylonian captivity the nation of Israel was divided into two kingdoms: Judah and Benjamin in the South (called the kingdom of Judah); and the other ten tribes in the North (called the kingdom of Israel). The kingdom of Judah, for the most part, returned to Palestine after the captivity, but the other ten tribes used the North Star as their guide. It was prophesied that the ten tribes would be scattered among many nations, thus they are called the Ten Lost Tribes (Jeremiah 13:24; 18:17; 49:32, Ezekiel 5:10,12; 1 Kings 22:17, etc.).

ALRISHA (the Band). This first decan of Pisces is the band that binds the two fish together. Yet the band is also tied to Cetus, the sea-monster representing Satan. Aries, the ram, represents Christ. The sign was originally a lamb (and still is in Hebrew), but the Romans changed it to a ram, considering the ram to be a more noble creature. Jesus is the Lamb of God. The paws of Aries are breaking the band that ties the fish to Cetus, and binding the monster with the band. What could this depict? The fish represent Judah (the Southern Kingdom) and Israel (the scattered Northern Kingdom). Christ Jesus suffered and died to break the bands that tie them to judgment.

> He brought them out of darkness and the shadow of death, and brake their bands in sunder (Psalm 107:14).

> Is not this the fast that I have chosen? to loose the bands of wickedness, to undo the heavy burdens, and to let the oppressed be free, and that ye break every yoke? (Isaiah 58:6)

ANDROMEDA (the Chained Woman). The Hebrews called this decan Sirra, the chained. The brightest stars are Mirach (the weak), and Desma (the bound). The sign is of a woman chained, a symbol of Israel, for that nation is likened to a woman (Revelation 12:1,2,5,6,13-17). It is Christ Jesus who breaks her binding chains.

The prophet Isaiah speaks of Israel as if that nation were a woman. Hosea 2:16-23 presents her as the wife of God. Israel is Zion, and the city of Jerusalem is the "Daughter of Zion":

> Therefore hear now this, thou afflicted, and drunken, but not with wine: Thus saith thy Lord the LORD, and thy God that pleadeth the cause of his people, Behold, I have taken out of thine hand the cup of trembling, even the dregs of the cup of my fury; thou shalt no more drink it again: But I will put it into the hand of them that afflict thee; which have said to thy soul, Bow down, that we may go over: and thou hast laid thy body as the ground, and as the street, to them that went over.

> Awake, awake; put on thy strength, O Zion; put on thy beautiful garments, O Jerusalem, the holy city: for henceforth there shall no more come into thee the uncircumcised and unclean. Shake thyself from the dust; arise, and sit down, O Jerusalem: loose thyself from the bands of thy neck, O captive daughter of Zion (Isaiah

51:21 – 52:2).

CEPHEUS (the Crowned King). Here is the presentation of a glorious king, crowned and enthroned in the highest heaven, with a scepter in his hand and his foot planted on the North Star. The brightest star is called Al Dermin, coming quickly. The king represents Christ: He shall return and reign as King of kings and Lord of lords (Psalms 5:2; 10:16; 24:7,9; 29:10; 47:7; 84:3; Isaiah 6:5; 33:17; 43:15; Jeremiah 23:5; Zechariah 9:9; Malachi 1:14; Matthew 25:34; Luke 19:38; John 1:49; 1 Timothy 1:17; Revelation 15:3). Other bright stars in this decan are called the redeemer, and the breaker.

The constellation of Pisces tells of the Southern and the Northern Kingdoms reunited, and the bands of death and Hell untied and broken by the Lamb and, as we shall see, the Breaker, Christ Jesus. The nation Israel is the chained woman, but has been set free by Christ, who shall come again as King of kings and Lord of lords.

## Aries: The Ram (Lamb)

The Hebrews called this constellation Taleh, the Lamb. The Romans changed the sign to a ram because they believed a ram to be a much more noble animal than a lamb. Yet, the original sign is that of a lamb, which is of course, the symbol of Jesus Christ:

> The next day John seeth Jesus coming unto him, and saith, Behold the Lamb of God, which taketh away the sin of the world (John 1:29).

Again the next day after John stood, and two of his disciples; And looking upon Jesus as he walked, he saith, Behold the Lamb of God! (John 1:35,36)

In the prophetic Book of the Revelation, John says the elders shall fall down "before the Lamb" and sing a new song saying:

Thou art worthy to take the book, and open the seals thereof: for thou wast slain, and hast redeemed us to God by thy blood out of every kindred, and tongue, and people, and nation (Revelation 5:9).

At that time John also heard angels and beasts and elders saying:

Worthy is the Lamb that was slain to receive power, and riches, and wisdom, and strength, and honour, and glory, and blessing (Revelation 5:12).

Christ is called the spotless Lamb, because He was a sinless sacrifice for sin. The brightest stars in Aries are called the slain, the bruised, and the pierced. Jesus was bruised for our iniquities, pierced for our transgressions, and slain to atone for our sins.

CASSIOPEIA (the Enthroned Woman). The Hebrews called this decan Schedir, the freed. Christ as the breaker broke the chains of death and Hell which had us bound, and as King He shall seat us upon His throne— He said:

To him that overcometh will I grant to sit with me in my throne, even as I also overcame, and am set down with my Father in his throne (Revelation 3:21).

Isaiah declares:

Thy Maker is thine husband; the LORD of hosts is his name; and thy Redeemer the Holy One of Israel; The God of the whole earth shall he be called. For the LORD hath called thee as a woman forsaken and grieved in spirit, and a wife of youth, when thou wast refused, saith thy God. For a small moment have I forsaken

thee; but with great mercies will I gather thee. In a little wrath I hid my face from thee for a moment; but
with everlasting kindness will I have mercy on thee,
saith the LORD thy Redeemer (Isaiah 54:5-8).

This is the Bride of Christ, the Lamb's wife, as John
declares:

Let us be glad and rejoice, and give honour to him: for
the marriage of the Lamb is come, and his wife hath
made herself ready (Revelation 19:7).

CETUS (the Sea-Monster). John saw the binding
of the old serpent which is the devil (and Satan), and he
saw him cast into the bottomless pit.

In this decan the sign is a sea-monster, the natural
enemy of the fishes. The brightest stars in this decan are
Menkar (bound enemy), Diphda (overthrown), and Mira
(rebel). When Jesus returns He will bind Satan for a
thousand years. At the end of that time the devil will be
loosened again, but Christ will destroy him — and his angels — completely. Isaiah declares:

In that day the LORD with his sore and great and strong
sword shall punish leviathan the piercing serpent, even
leviathan that crooked serpent; and he shall slay the
dragon that is in the sea (Isaiah 27:1).

PERSEUS (the Breaker). The Hebrews call this
decan Peretz, the breaker.

This is the very same word used for Christ in the
Old Testament:

The breaker is come up before them: they have broken
up, and have passed through the gate, and are gone out
by it: and their king shall pass before them, and the
LORD on the head of them (Micah 2:13).

Perseus holds in his right hand his "sore and great
and strong sword," lifted up to smite and break down the
enemy. He has wings on his feet and is the angel ascending from the east "having the seal of the living God"

(Revelation 7:2). The brightest star in this decan is called he who breaks. The sign in the heavens is that of a man with a sword breaking the chains that bind Andromeda, the chained woman. It is Jesus that sets free the woman (the nation Israel) from the chains of death and Hell.

The head Perseus carries in his left hand is called Medusa by the Greeks, the Hebrew root of which means the trodden under foot. It is also called Rosh Satan, the head of the adversary. While Perseus breaks the chains of the woman He also bruises the head of His enemy. This is what the "seed of the woman" was to do to Satan, according to Genesis 3.

The constellation of Aries tells of the Lamb (Aries) that shall deliver the enthroned woman (Cassiopeia) from the sea-monster who is Satan (Cetus) by breaking the chains of Hell and death that have kept Andromeda bound. The breaker is Perseus (Christ).

## Taurus: The Ox

The sign in the heavens is that of an ox, or bull, rushing forward with mighty energy and fierce wrath; his horns are to push his enemies and pierce them through to destroy them. In Hebrew this constellation is called Shur, the ruler.

Among the sons of Israel was Joseph. He is known as a "type of Christ." Joseph's brothers sold him into slavery because he had a prophetic dream in which he was told he would rule over his brethren.

Jesus was betrayed into the hands of the Romans because He would be king. Joseph was put in prison for a crime he was not guilty of, then later was made viceroy of Egypt. Jesus died the death of a criminal, but He was sinless. In the last days He shall rule over all the earth.

Job is asked, "Canst thou bind the sweet influences of Pleiades?" (Job 38:31, also mentioned in Job 9:9). The Pleiades are the "seven stars," a cluster of stars found somewhere in the zodiac. Which constellation would they be in?

Within Taurus is a cluster of seven stars called the Pleides; these are mentioned in Amos 5:8. The brightest stars are called Kimah (congregation) and Palilicium (belonging to the judge). In Revelation, John writes to the seven angels, or messengers, of the seven churches (Revelation 1:16; 2:1). Is not the church the "congregation" that "belongs to the judge"?

To understand Taurus we must look at the blessing of Jacob upon his son Joseph:

> His glory is like the firstlings of his bullock, and his horns are like the horns of unicorns: with them he shall push the people together to the ends of the earth (Deuteronomy 33:17).

Jesus told us that before His return God would send His angels for the gathering of the House of Israel:

> And he shall send his angels with a great sound of a trumpet, and they shall gather together his elect from the four winds, from one end of heaven to the other (Matthew 24:31).

ORION (the Dayspring). The name comes from a Hebrew root word which means dayspring or dawning. In several places Jesus is called the light of the world (for example, see John 8:12 and 9:5). He also is called the Sun of Righteousness:

But unto you that fear my name shall the Sun of righteousness arise with healing in his wings; and ye shall go forth, and grow up as calves of the stall. And ye shall tread down the wicked; for they shall be as ashes under the soles of your feet in the day that I shall do this, saith the LORD of hosts (Malachi 4:2,3).

Jesus came as that Sun of Righteousness:

Through the tender mercy of our God; whereby the dayspring from on high hath visited us, to give light to them that sit in darkness and in the shadow of death, to guide our feet into the way of peace (Luke 1:78,79).

The picture in the heavens is that of a man holding a lion's head in one hand and a club in the other, his left foot crushing the head of Lepus, the rabbit, and a stream of fire flowing from that foot. The head he is crushing with the club represents the head of Satan, for Peter says,

Be sober, be vigilant; because your adversary the devil, as a roaring lion, walketh about, seeking whom he may devour (1 Peter 5:8).

The brightest stars in this decan are Betelgeux (the coming branch), Bellatrix (coming swiftly), Al Nitak (the wounded), and Saiph (bruised) – the very word used in Genesis 3:15.

ERIDANUS (the River of the Judge). The river of fire that flows from the foot of Orion runs downward until it consumes Cetus, the sea-monster. In a vision Daniel saw a "fiery stream that issued and came forth from before him." This is the river of the judge, for Daniel continues, "The judgement was set, and the books were opened." (See Daniel 7:9-11.) Psalm 97 describes the scene when the Lord shall reign:

A fire goeth before him, and burneth up his enemies round about (Psalm 97:3).

Other biblical passages also describe this event:

Our God shall come, and shall not keep silence: a fire shall devour before him, and it shall be very tempestuous round about him (Psalm 50:3).

And to you who are troubled rest with us, when the Lord Jesus shall be revealed from heaven with his mighty angels, In flaming fire taking vengeance on them that know not God, and that obey not the gospel of our Lord Jesus Christ (2 Thessalonians 1:7,8).

AURIGA (the Shepherd). The third decan of Taurus is Auriga, the shepherd. The Lord is referred to as a "shepherd" in the Bible:

Behold, the Lord GOD will come with strong hand, and his arm shall rule for him: behold, his reward is with him, and his work before him. He shall feed his flock like a shepherd: he shall gather the lambs with his arm, and carry them in his bosom, and shall gently lead those that are with young (Isaiah 40:10,11).

The sign in the heavens is a shepherd gently holding a kid across one shoulder. The brightest star is called Alioth: meaning she-goat in Hebrew. In the right foot is a star called El Nath (the wounded). Christ Jesus is the Shepherd who loves His sheep and gave His life for them. He said:

I am the good shepherd: the good shepherd giveth his life for the sheep . . . I am the good shepherd, and know my sheep, and am known of mine (John 10:11,14).

The constellation of Taurus tells the story of the congregation of the judge (Taurus) that shall spread the gospel and gather the believers. They do this to await the judge, the one called dayspring. When this judge comes He shall destroy the wicked by fire (Eridanus), and gather His flock to Himself (the Shepherd).

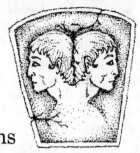

# Gemini: The Twins

The Hebrews called this constellation Thaumim, united. The sign in the heavens is two men of war who are twins. They are not battling but walking hand in hand in peace. There is a bright star in each head; one is called Ruler, and the other is Propus (the spreading branch). The Twins represent the united kingdoms of Judah and Israel in the last days. How do we know this? As we have seen, the two Southern tribes became the kingdom of Judah. The Northern ten tribes were known as Ephraim or Israel and through captivity were scattered among the Gentile, heathen nations. The head of the Northern Kingdom was always Ephraim. Before their captivity, these two kingdoms constantly battled each another, but in the last days they shall be reunited:

> The envy also of Ephraim shall depart, and the adversaries of Judah shall be cut off: Ephraim shall not envy Judah, and Judah shall not vex Ephraim (Isaiah 11:13).

Judah is to be the house of the ruler:

> The scepter shall not depart from Judah, nor a lawgiver from between his feet, until Shiloh come; and unto him shall the gathering of the people be (Genesis 49:10).

The Northern Kingdom would spread throughout the Gentile nations like a "spreading branch":

> Joseph is a fruitful bough, even a fruitful bough by a well; whose branches run over the wall (Genesis 49:22).

At the time of the Assyrian (2 Kings 17:4-6) and Babylonian (2 Chronicles 36:15-21) captivities, the scattering of the Jews began. It was finalized at the destruction of the Temple in Jerusalem in 70 A.D. and it continued into our century. Men who believed in the Bible proclaimed that God would gather all the Jews into the Holy Land again, but the world did not believe them. Yet, in 1948 the reestablishment of Israel as a recognized nation became a reality. God promised that in the last days He would gather Israel (the ten tribes scattered among the Gentiles) to Himself. This is in fulfillment of prophecy:

> Thus saith the Lord GOD; Behold I will take the children of Israel from among the heathen, whither they be gone, and will gather them on every side, and bring them into their own land (Ezekiel 37:21).

In the last day Israel and Judah shall be united again upon the everlasting hills:

> And I will make them one nation in the land upon the mountains of Israel; and one king shall be king to them all: and they shall be no more two nations, neither shall they be divided into two kingdoms any more at all (Ezekiel 37:22).

LEPUS (the Hare). The brightest stars in the decan are called the deceiver, the mad, and the bound. The very brightest star is named in the Hebrew, Arnebo, the enemy. Just as the mighty man crushes the scorpion, so Orion (the dayspring) is shown crushing Lepus. Scorpio represents the seed of the serpent, conflict and war, and enmity. This means that when Christ returns He shall end war and conflict. He shall establish peace. Here we see Orion, or Christ, crushing another enemy. Yet, what could such an innocent animal like the hare represent?

In the immoral fertility cults of the ancients the hare, or rabbit, represented fertility (need you ask why?), and Israel was constantly falling into apostasy as a result of observing the abominable rites of those cults. The Bible tells us that sexual immorality is an abomination before God (Leviticus 18). The effects of sexual immorality cause plagues, and the ultimate destruction of homes, families and nations. Just as war and conflict will end when Christ returns, so will the wickedness of sexual immorality:

> Upon the wicked he shall rain snares, fire and brimstone, and an horrible tempest: this shall be the portion of their cup (Psalm 11:6).

> Through God we shall do valiantly: for he it is that shall tread down our enemies (Psalm 60:12).

The Bible, God's revelation to man, condemns sex outside of marriage (Jude 7), homosexuality (1 Corinthians 6:9), bestiality (Leviticus 18:23), adultery (Exodus 20:14) and transvestitism (Deuteronomy 22:5). God says He will punish the wicked who engage in these sins. Yet, He also offered His own Son to suffer for those sins, and to provide a way of salvation for any sinner who will repent and follow Him.

CANIS MAJOR (the Big Dog). The Hebrews called this decan Zeeb: the wolf. The picture is that of a wolf pleading for mercy. The mouth of the wolf is shut by Sirius, the prince. The Romans changed this sign to a dog because they had a legend of a great hunter who had two hunting dogs which went before him. They thought Orion was the great hunter so they changed the signs of the wolf and the lamb into Canis Major and Canis Minor. These two decans can only be understood together. Jesus, who is the Prince of Peace, shall shut the mouth of the wolf. The symbol of the wolf meant greediness. How many wars have been waged over the greediness of a few? At the last day peace shall reign over the earth because of the Prince of Peace:

> The wolf also shall dwell with the lamb, and the leopard shall lie down with the kid; and the calf and the young

lion and the fatling together; and a little child shall lead them (Isaiah 11:6).

CANIS MINOR (the Little Dog). Originally this was the sign of a lamb. The brightest star in this decan is named Exalted Redeemer.

The story of Gemini is the story of how Ephraim (the scattered Northern Kingdom of Israel) and Judah (the Southern Kingdom) shall be reunited in peace. When the Dayspring (Orion) returns He shall crush sexual immorality (Lepus), and cause the wolf (Canis Major) to lie down with the lamb (Canis Minor). Jesus is the Prince (Sirius) of Peace (Isaiah 9:6).

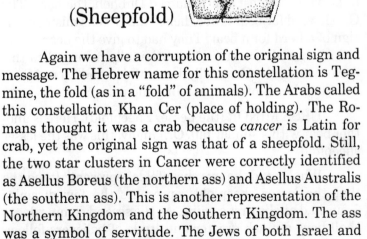

# Cancer:
# The Crab
# (Sheepfold)

Again we have a corruption of the original sign and message. The Hebrew name for this constellation is Tegmine, the fold (as in a "fold" of animals). The Arabs called this constellation Khan Cer (place of holding). The Romans thought it was a crab because *cancer* is Latin for crab, yet the original sign was that of a sheepfold. Still, the two star clusters in Cancer were correctly identified as Asellus Boreus (the northern ass) and Asellus Australis (the southern ass). This is another representation of the Northern Kingdom and the Southern Kingdom. The ass was a symbol of servitude. The Jews of both Israel and Judah were to be His servants, His sheep.

It was foretold that the Messiah would come riding upon an ass followed by the colt of an ass:

Rejoice greatly, O daughter of Zion; shout, O daughter of Jerusalem: behold, thy King cometh unto thee: he is just, and having salvation; lowly, and riding upon an ass, and upon a colt of the foal of an ass (Zechariah 9:9).

And the disciples went, and did as Jesus commanded them, And brought the ass, and the colt, and put on them their clothes, and they set him thereon. And a very great multitude spread their garments in the way; others cut down branches from the trees, and strewed them in the way. And the multitude that went before, and that followed, cried, saying, Hosanna to the Son of David: Blessed is he that cometh in the name of the Lord; Hosanna in the highest (Matthew 21:6-9).

In the center of this constellation is a bright cluster of stars called Praesepe, the multitude.

URSA MAJOR (the Greater Sheepfold). Again we have a corruption of the original sign, for the sign in the heavens as depicted in charts now is that of a bear with a large, long tail. The problem is, bears do not have such tails. The brightest star is named Dubheh, the herd. The Greek word for bear is *dob;* hence the Greeks mistook this sign of a herd for a bear. They had to give the bear a long tail so that all the stars that originally belonged to this decan would fit. Originally Ursa Major and Ursa Minor were two herds of sheep circling the polestar.

URSA MINOR (the Lesser Sheepfold). Here is another bear with a similar tail. Originally, this was the lesser sheepfold.

What could the two sheepfolds represent? It may be that the lesser sheepfold represents the few disciples Jesus had at His first coming. At His second coming Jesus shall have a much greater multitude of believers following Him. This would explain the greater and the lesser sheepfolds. It may mean that the lesser fold refers to Judah (the Southern Kingdom), and the greater fold refers to the Northern Kingdom. The Lord said:

> As a shepherd seeketh out his flock in the day that he is among his sheep that are scattered; so will I seek out my sheep, and will deliver them out of all places where they have been scattered in the cloudy and dark day (Ezekiel 34:12).

Jesus also said that He had "other sheep," John 10:16: "And other sheep I have which are not of this fold: them also I must bring." Could the prophet Ezekiel be referring to these other sheep as the believing Gentiles?

There are twenty-four stars in these two decans. They are the closest ones to the polestar. This is called Polaris or the North Star. From the earth, it seems that the entire universe revolves around this central star.

> And round about the throne were four and twenty seats: and upon the seats I saw four and twenty elders sitting, clothed in white raiment; and they had on their heads crowns of gold (Revelation 4:4).

ARGO (the Ship). The third decan of Cancer is Argo, the ship. We see the sign in the heavens as a ship. The ship represents the redeemed. The Hebrew name for this decan is the Redeemed:

> Art thou not it which hath dried the sea, the waters of the great deep; that hath made the depths of the sea a way for the ransomed to pass over? (Isaiah 51:10)

The constellation of Cancer tells the story of the sheepfolds of the Redeemer. The Good Shepherd died to ransom His sheep. We are His servants and His sheep. The sheep are held in His fold, and He has made a way for them to pass over the sea of death and Hell.

# Leo:
# The Lion

The twelfth and last constellation along the path of the sun is called in Latin, Leo, and in Hebrew, Arieh. Both mean lion. The sign in the heavens is a mighty lion with his feet over the serpent Hydra. The brightest stars are called Regulus (treading under foot), Denebola (the judge cometh), and Deneb Aleced (the judge shall reign). Balaam foretold:

> God brought him forth out of Egypt; he hath as it were the strength of an unicorn: he shall eat up the nations of his enemies, and shall break their bones, and pierce them through with his arrows. He couched, he lay down as a lion, and as a great lion: who shall stir him up? (Numbers 24:8,9)

In John's Book of the Revelation we discover just who the lion represents:

> And one of the elders saith unto me, Weep not: behold, the Lion of the tribe of Juda, the Root of David, hath prevailed to open the book, and to loose the seven seals thereof. And I beheld, and, lo, in the midst of the throne and of the four beasts, and in the midst of the elders, stood a Lamb as it had been slain, having seven horns and seven eyes, which are the seven spirits of God sent forth into all the earth. And he came and took the book out of the right hand of him that sat upon the throne. And when he had taken the book, the four beasts and four and twenty elders fell down before the Lamb, having every one of them harps, and golden vials full of odours, which are the prayers of saints. And they

sung a new song, saying, Thou art worthy to take the book, and to open the seals thereof: for thou wast slain, and hast redeemed us to God by thy blood out of every kindred, and tongue, and people, and nation; And hath made us unto our God kings and priests: and we shall reign on the earth (Revelation 5:5-10).

HYDRA (the Serpent). The sign in the heavens is a fleeing serpent. The brightest stars are called the deceiver and the abhorred. On the back of the serpent is a cup or bowl and a raven; these are the other two decans of Leo. The fleeing serpent, of course, represents Satan.

CRATER (the Cup). The second decan is seen as a cup or bowl filled with fire ready to be poured out onto the serpent. Hydra also represents the wicked, and the cup represents the wrath of God that shall be poured out upon the wicked at the last day:

> For in the hand of the Lord there is a cup, and the wine is red; it is full of mixture; and he poureth out of the same: but the dregs thereof, all the wicked of the earth shall wring them out, and drink them (Psalm 75:8).

> Upon the wicked he shall rain snares, fire and brimstone, and an horrible tempest: this shall be the portion of their cup (Psalm 11:6).

> The same shall drink of the wine of the wrath of God, which is poured out without mixture into the cup of his indignation; and he shall be tormented with fire and brimstone in the presence of the holy angels, and in the presence of the Lamb (Revelation 14:10).

CORVUS (the Raven). Here is a picture of a raven tearing into the fleeing serpent. The end of all warfare and wickedness is depicted in the Bible with the fowls of the air clearing away the carnage. In the Bible ravens are said to punish the wicked:

> The eye that mocketh at his father, and despiseth to obey his mother, the ravens of the valley shall pick it out, and the young eagles shall eat it (Proverbs 30:17).

And I saw an angel standing in the sun; and he cried with a loud voice, saying to all the fowls that fly in the midst of heaven, Come and gather yourselves together unto the supper of the great God; That ye may eat the flesh of kings and the flesh of captains, and the flesh of mighty men, and the flesh of horses, and of them that sit on them, and the flesh of all men, both free and bond, both small and great (Revelation 19:17,18).

The story of the constellation of Leo gives the message of the Lion of Judah who shall trample upon the wicked at His coming. He shall pour out His cup of wrath upon those who do wickedly, and the birds of the air shall punish them. Thus we see the representations that at the Day of Judgment the wicked may try to flee, but they shall not escape judgment.

# III Astrology: Science or Superstition?

In the previous chapters we have seen how the heavens declare the glory of God. We have decoded the secret message of the zodiac. What does the message reveal? It reveals the person of Jesus of Nazareth. Now we can reconstruct the original meaning of the zodiac:

1. Virgo: The virgin shall conceive and bear a son who is called the branch and the seed of the woman.

2. Libra: The son shall pay the price for sin.

3. Scorpio: He shall crush the seed of the serpent.

4. Sagittarius: He shall conquer sin and death.

5. Capricornus: He shall die to atone for sin so that the fish may live.

6. Aquarius: He shall pour forth streams of living water for the dying fish.

7. Pisces: He shall set the captives free.

8. Aries: He shall be the Lamb of God.

9. Taurus: He shall gather His elect from the four winds.

10.  Gemini: He shall reunite the nations in peace.

11.  Cancer: He shall take His sheep to Himself.

12.  Leo: He shall reign as a lion, and punish the wicked at the final day.

We have seen that the zodiac is a clear and unmistakable message of Christ Jesus. Why hasn't astrology, which is supposed to be the receptacle of this secret knowledge, told us about this message? According to astrology the signs don't mean anything. Also, no astrologist today even uses the 36 decans. Yet, aren't they there for a purpose? They indeed are, and we have seen it.

This brings us to the next inevitable question: Is astrology true, or is it a corruption of a truth long lost to the world?

In this chapter we shall make a study of astrology from two views: scientific and scriptural.

## Astrology Vs. Science

We first find astrology in the ancient cities of the Babylonian plains. After that, the chief architect of astrology was the Greek philosopher and occultist Ptolemy. He developed astrology with all of its ancient "scientific" criteria. He wrote that the earth was the center of the universe, and the sun, moon, stars and five planets (only five were visible to the naked eye) circled the earth and focused certain powers that determined human destiny.

During the Dark Ages astrology thrived. Most of the popes had in-house astrologers. When the Dark Ages became the "Golden Age," astrology began to decline. Scientists discovered that the earth was not the center of the universe, and the sun, moon and stars did not revolve around the earth—but astrologers simply ignored that fact. Their entire belief system was based on these heavenly bodies revolving around the earth. Their response to the new knowledge was typical: They acted like all was "business as usual." Later, when four more planets were discovered (Mercury, Neptune, Uranus and Pluto), astrologers either conveniently "added" them or ignored them. This leads to the question, If planets influence the earth, and if these four planets were there before they were discovered, wouldn't they also influence the earth?

Some of the statistics about astrology in this country, and elsewhere, are startling. According to Gallup polls taken during the past twenty years the influence of astrology is staggering. Here are just a few examples:

(1975) 32 million Americans believed in astrology.[1] That figure is much greater today.

(1984) 55 percent of American teenagers believe in astrology.[2]

(1988) 10 percent of those claiming to be evangelical Christians believe in astrology.[3]

Surprisingly few people realize there are as many astrologists in Western society as there are psychologists.[4] Horoscopes can be found in 80 percent of American newspapers.[5] In 1969 alone, for example, the American public spent over $150 million on personal horoscope material.[6]

Astrology in Europe is even stronger than in the United States. Christian cult-watcher William J. Petersen reports:

> In Great Britain, more than two-thirds of the adult population read their horoscopes. In France 53 percent read their horoscopes daily, and in Germany the percentage who take astrology somewhat seriously is 63.[7]

The occultic arts are gaining acceptance in the West

at an alarming rate – largely because the practitioners of these rites pawn them off as *scientific*. This is true of all Aquarian rites and practices, including the occultic art of astrology. The claims of these astrologists are typical:

### Gary Keen

Astrology is a system of scientific calculation. The interpretations that derive from this are based on traditional empirical references that have established their validity through centuries of time.[8]

### June Wakefield

Astrology is a science. It is not a pseudo-science.[9]

### John Manolesco

I have never heard of a single person who attacked astrology on real scientific grounds.[10]

A good number of studies have been done through the years to prove or disprove astrology. The American Association of Scientific Societies investigated studies done by astrologists who claimed their studies "proved" astrology to be true. The scientists came to the conclusion that "none of the influences alleged by the astrologers was verified."[11]

The joust between astrologist and scientist has by no means been limited to the U.S. Back in the early '70s a Swiss astrologist by the name of Robur claimed to have amassed a great amount of evidence showing how musicians had the same astrological sun-sign. Robur created such a stir that a French astronomer, by the name of Paul Carderc, decided to evaluate Robur's evidence. After much investigation Carderc declared:

NO sign of the zodiac or fraction of a sign favors or does not favor them. We conclude: The assets of scientific astrology are equal to zero, as is the case with commercial astrology.[12]

Another astrologist claimed, as many do, that artists are predominately Libras. One American scientist painstakingly studied the birthdates of thousands of artists, and discovered that not only was there no correlation, but also that "Libra had fewer than its quota of artists."[13]

Astrologists claim that the sign we are born under determines our personality traits. In the mid '70s two psychologists designed a test for students and faculty to rate themselves on a list of personality traits. After the study, the psychologists concluded:

> Analysis of the results found no tie between the subject's self-description, their friends' description or their rating on the psychological test and characteristics ascribed to them by their horoscopes.[14]

## Astro-Twins

Most of us have seen and read the supermarket tabloids. Browsing through them offers many of us a brief and humorous respite from the dull drudgery of a long and limping check-out line. Right under the headline, "I Bore an Alien's Two-Headed Love Child," you'll find articles like, "Twins Separated From Birth Win Lottos in Different States," and, "A Thousand Miles Apart but a Thousand Ways Alike." These articles tell about "astro-twins," people, related or not, who are born at the very same moment. According to astrology they would *have* to lead identical lives. Astrologist J. Goodavage comments:

> People with identical horoscopes will live parallel lives and experience many things in common. This is proof of the validity of astrology.[15]

A non-Christian, by the name of Keith Eriksen, decided to do a thorough investigation of astro-twin case studies for the *Humanist* magazine.[16] Here are synopses of several cases he studied:

**Case #1** (from *Horoscope* magazine, May 1976)

Donald Chapman and Donald Brazill were born in California. Each boy came into the world at almost the same moment on September 5, 1933, in neighborhood towns about twenty-four miles apart.

Five days after their twenty-third birthday on September 10, 1956, Don Brazill of Ferndale and Don Chapman of Eureka met for the first and last time in this life. They were driving in opposite directions on U.S. Highway 101 south of Eureka early on a Sunday morning after taking their girlfriends (who live in each others' hometown!) home when their cars crashed head-on. Both were killed instantly—decapitated.

FACTS

1. The men were born 3-1/2 hours apart.

2. Neither was decapitated. One died of a crushed skull, and the other a cerebral hemorrhage.

Many will say, "Doesn't this prove astrology?" No, because these two men were not born at the very same moment (which makes an astro-twin). If astro-twins were those born on the same day, then, according to astrology, everyone born on that day and year should have been killed by a blow to the head when the two young men were. No, it was a coincidence that the two men were born on the same day. Coincidences do happen. This is not even a case of astro-twins.

**Case #2** (from *Astrology: The Space Age Science,* p. 32)

In 1939 two unrelated women met for the first time in a hospital room in Hackensack, New Jersey. Their last names were Hanna and Osborne, but they had the same first name, Edna. Each woman had a baby at the same time; the babies weighed the same and were given the same name, Patricia Edna.

Just another coincidence? Maybe, but here's what their conversation revealed. Both their husbands were named Harold. Each Harold was in the same business and owned the same make, model and color car. The Hannas and Osbornes had been married exactly three and a half years and had the same anniversary. The babies were their first. Both fathers were born in the same year, month and day. The mothers too had the same birth date and the same number of brothers and sisters. Each Edna was a blue-eyed brunette, same height, same weight and wore the same kind of clothes. Their husbands were of the same religion, a different one from that of the wives, which was also the same. Each family owned a dog named Spot, same mixed breed, same size, and the same age. Both Spots were bought at the same time and were of the same sex.

FACTS (obtained from Mrs. H. B. Hanna)

1. The babies were born more than an hour apart.
2. The fathers were not in the same business.
3. The fathers did not own the same make, model or color car.
4. The couples did not have the same marriage anniversary.
5. The fathers were not born on the same day, month or year.
6. The mothers did not share the same birth date.

**Case #3** (from "The Strange Mystery of Astro-Twins," *Science and Mechanics,* March 1967)

It seems that every astrologer in New York City was aware of the fact that the city's former top two commissioners—police: Michael J. Murphy, and fire: Edward Thompson—were born within an hour of each other on July 19, 1913, in the same neighborhood of Queensborough . . .

Each man attended many of the same schools at the same times, including Brooklyn Law School. Both graduated in 1936, but from then on . . . a 12-month interval separated major, similar events in their careers.

Thus when Commissioner Thompson resigned to take another post, it seemed . . . by use of astrology, that Police Commissioner Murphy would be out of office within the year. It worked out in the most uncanny way, right on the click of the planetary "dials," you would say.

FACTS (obtained from Edward Thompson)

1.  Mr. Thompson says that no one knows the exact time of his birth.

2.  Mr. Thompson graduated from law school in 1936. Murphy graduated in 1938.

Again, we don't know if we have astro-twins here. Many of the young Irish men from that neighborhood joined the police and fire departments of New York City. The high achievers among them earned graduate degrees. It should not surprise us that two of them became commissioners.

**Case #4** (from *Astrology: The Space Age Science*, p. 33)

On March 30, 1964, a doctor and his wife were sentenced to two years in prison in Tucson, Arizona, for extreme cruelty to their five-year-old adopted daughter, Tina. The child was found by the housekeeper, beaten, bloody and half-starved. Her hands were tightly roped around her back and she cowered behind the furnace room in the basement . . .

At almost the same time, but in another state, an identical story unfolded. A dentist and his wife had beaten and brutalized their five-year-old adopted daughter and kept her tied up in the basement of their home. They too were sentenced.

The second child was Tina's twin sister from whom she had been separated since infancy!

FACTS (obtained from Tucson Star newspaper reference librarian)

1.  Tina's twin was a male.

2. The twin brother died more than a year and a half before Tina was found badly beaten.

3. The twin brother had never been separated from the family; the story of the dentist and his wife was a total fabrication.

This actually was a story of how a doctor and his wife abused one twin, a boy, to death, and a year and a half later nearly killed the other twin, a girl. Astrologists fabricated a lot for this story in order to "prove" astrology true. This is actually the first confirmed case of "astro-twins" we have seen. It only proves that the astrological belief that astro-twins will have the same life and fate is erroneous.

**Case #5** (from "The Strange Mystery of Astro-Twins," *Science and Mechanics,* March 1967)

In Philadelphia's Jefferson Medical College, Drs. Thomas D. Duane and Thomas Behrendt performed an exciting experiment with fifteen sets of twins. In separate, brilliantly lit rooms, the twins were wired to electro-encephalograph machines which produced a perfectly identifiable brain-wave pattern called the Alpha rhythm. One twin was told to blink his eyes each time he asked. The other twin of course had no idea what was going on and wasn't told anything about the experiment's purpose. Yet in almost all cases, the twin who did nothing at all registered the identical brain wave "sent" by the twin who was blinking his eyes!

FACT (obtained from Dr. T. Duane)

Results showed only 2 of 15 sets of twins registered identical brain wave patterns.

Even if all sets of twins had shown identical brain waves, how does this prove astrology? The astrologists claim they would have the same lives and fates; not the same brain waves! Astrologists love to stack and fabricate evidence, and then argue from positions that could not possibly support their case in the first place.[17]

Probably the most knowledgeable and famous person to study astrology from a scientific point of view is French scientist Michel Gauquelin. He started as a supporter of astrology, and many astrologists still quote his initial opinions. Yet Gauquelin found that "facts are stubborn things." He later became the author of such works as *The Scientific Basis of Astrology: Myth and Reality*[18] and *Dreams and Illusions of Astrology*.[19] The French scientist could not have been more fair. Most of his studies came at astrologists' requests; they wanted him to confirm their beliefs.[20] After many years of working with astrologists, Michel Gauquelin came to this conclusion:

> Every attempt, whether of astrologers or scientists, to produce the evidence of the validity of astrological laws has been in vain. It is now quite certain that the signs in the sky which presided over our births have no power whatever to decide our fates, to affect our hereditary characteristics, or play any part however humble in the totality of affects, random and otherwise, which form the fabric of our lives and mold our impulses to action. Confronted with science, modern and traditional astrology are seen to be imaginary doctrines.[21]

Researcher Robert Eisler remarked that astrologists "will not acknowledge honestly the decisive fact that their futile practices have been investigated with the greatest care and impartiality by the foremost scholars of the leading Western nations for almost three centuries, and not one of these has failed to condemn them."[22]

It isn't easy to convince a believer in astrology that it isn't true. *Time* magazine reported this enigma:

> There are so many variables and options to play with that the astrologer is always right. Break a leg when your astrologer told you the signs were good, and

he can congratulate you on escaping what might have happened had the signs been bad. Conversely, if you go against the signs and nothing happens, the astrologer can insist that you were subconsciously careful because you were forewarned.[23]

Astrologers will ignore, cover up and disregard all evidence to the contrary, and they will keep saying astrology is scientific. Now, you know better. Science has proven astrology false. If astrologists want to hold it as a religion, fine, but don't call it scientific! Astrology is a pseudo (false) science. Indeed, the apostle Paul warns us against all the occultic arts, which he terms "science falsely so-called" (1 Timothy 6:20).

## Astrology Vs. the Bible

Astrologers, and their followers the astrologists, claim that the Bible is on their side, and that it is the Christians who misunderstand the Bible. Let's see what a few noted astrologers have to say, and compare it with what the Bible has to say.

### Karma

*Ronald Davison*

[The gospel] is the story of the most perfect Being whosoever incarnated on earth [and] tells of the ultimate sacrifice on the cross . . . for the purpose of paying off any remaining debts of his own to the past.[24]

This sounds, at first, complementary to Jesus and the Bible. But wait. Notice Davison said Jesus was crucified to pay back *His own* Karmic debts. What are Karmic debts? Here's the answer: Aquarianity (a new term for the entire body of world view beliefs that are in contrast to Christianity) teaches that we all reincarnate over and over again. We do this to rid our souls of Karma (really, *all* Karma is bad so I don't refer to "good" and "bad"

Karma). We rid ourselves of Karma by *suffering*. Life in matter is seen as a mistake, and to rid ourselves of Karma, which keeps us matter-bound, we must go through pain and death, and all other forms of suffering. This takes many lifetimes, but it is necessary for the soul to free itself of matter.

We may liken it, say, to a child who wears his new clothes out to play. After play his clothes are very dirty. He cannot go to school unless his clothes are cleaned. It takes many washes to get all the stains out. Our souls, according to the doctrine of reincarnation, are like the dirty clothes. Our suffering in life is the cleansing process, but life also collects Karma (like the child at play again). The Hindus and Buddhists call this the Wheel of Rebirth. We are here over and over again in order to suffer and learn so that our lives may be more fortunate in the next incarnation. All reincarnationists believe that eventually they escape from the Wheel of Rebirth and enter Nirvana, a state of divine bliss — or of becoming one with the cosmos. Their belief says that at that time a person is no longer a part of the material realm but has entered a spiritual kingdom and become one with that realm as a drop of rain becomes one with the ocean.

Astrologer Davison says that Jesus went to the cross to pay back some of "His own" Karmic debt left over from a previous incarnation.

THE BIBLE

Jesus could not have paid off previous Karma (prior sins) because He was God (John 1:1,3,14). The apostle John wrote:

> Whosoever committeth sin transgresseth also the law: for sin is the transgression of the law. And ye know that he was manifested to take away our sins; and in him is no sin (1 John 3:4,5).

The Bible says that (1) Jesus paid for our sins, and (2) Jesus was God and therefore had no sins. Astrologer Davison said the exact opposite!

## The Scriptures

### Nicholas De Vore

Either the Christian religion is astrology, or astrology is the source of the Christian religion; for there is no conflict between them. Both Old and New Testaments abound in astrological symbolism and teachings.[25]

### Jeff Mayo

The Bible is full of astrological references.[26]

THE BIBLE

As we have seen, the Bible is full of references to the Mazzaroth. Perhaps it would be better to say that the Mazzaroth is full of references and symbolisms that are found in the Bible! Astrology, which is the occultic art of forecasting events by the movements of the heavens, is *condemned* throughout the Bible. Here are several examples:

If there be found among you, within any of the gates which the LORD thy God giveth thee, man or woman, that hath wrought wickedness in the sight of the LORD thy God, in transgressing his covenant, And hath gone and served other gods, and worshipped them, either the sun, or moon, or any of the host of heaven, which I have not commanded; And it be told thee, and thou hast heard of it, and enquired diligently, and, behold, it be true, and the thing certain, that such abomination is wrought in Israel: Then shalt thou bring forth that man or that woman, which have committed that wicked thing, unto thy gates, even that man or that woman, and shalt stone them with stones, till they die (Deuteronomy 17:2-5).

Isaiah says to Babylon that they have trusted in their wickedness, and that "thy wisdom and thy knowledge, it hath perverted thee" (47:10). He promises them that "desolation shall come upon thee suddenly" (v. 11). Isaiah challenges them to stand with their sorceries in order to try to escape wrath (he is being sarcastic here). He writes:

> Let now the astrologers, the stargazers, the monthly prognosticators, stand up, and save thee from these things that shall come upon thee. Behold, they shall be as stubble; the fire shall burn them; they shall not deliver themselves from the power of the flame (Isaiah 47:13,14).

The people of Babylon had trusted in astrology, and followed the wicked advice they had received. God would punish Babylon, and Isaiah mocks them saying, "Okay, you put so much trust in astrology—let's see if it can save you from your doom!" It didn't.

Moses declared in Deuteronomy that the Lord commanded him to give statutes and laws to Israel so that they would *not* (1) corrupt themselves with graven images; or (2) lift up their eyes to heaven, and "be driven to worship" the stars (Deuteronomy 4:16,19).

**God**

Here are comments by astrologers on God:

*Arthur Dione*

God dwells in you as You.[27]

*Alice O. Howell*

Everything, everything is God![28]

*Irene Diamond*

I am God.[29]

*Alan Oken*

Humanity as a whole IS the Messiah.[30]

THE BIBLE

Astrologers believe that the cosmos (universe) is God, and that man is God since man is the highest evolved species in the cosmos. However, if man had been God, then God would not have said:

> God is not a man, that he should lie; neither the Son of man, that he should repent (Numbers 23:19).

Indeed, if we were all the Messiah then Jesus would *not* have needed to say, "I am the way, the truth, and the life: no man cometh unto the Father, but by me" (John 14:6).

No, the occultic pseudo-science of astrology and Christianity are as opposite as black and white. One is from Lucifer, and the other is from Jehovah.

Some astrologers claim that early Christianity taught openly of astrology but that later the Bible was changed. There is absolutely no evidence for this. In fact, the earliest biblical manuscripts are consistent. None of them teach astrology. In the *Didache,* written by Christians who sat at the feet of the apostles of Jesus, we read:

> My child, be no dealer in omens, since it leads to idolatry, nor an enchanter, nor an astrologer, nor a magician, neither be willing to look at them; for from all these things idolatry is engendered.[31]

## Astrology and Prophecy

Astrologers' claim to fame is that they can, through astrology, predict the future. We will discuss this more in a later chapter, but here are a few points to consider now:

1. Astrologers predicted that in 1982 a conjunction of planets (the Jupiter effect) would cause major catastrophes. Nothing unusual occurred in 1982.[32]

2. Not one astrologer could predict World War II. After it started, all agreed that Great Britain would remain neutral.[33] Wrong on both counts.

3. Astrologers predicted that the Communist government of Red China would fall by 1970.[34] It didn't.

4. Astrologers predicted that California would fall into the ocean in 1969.[35] California has yet to do this.

5. A number of astrologers predicted that John Glenn would be President in 1988.[36] George Bush became President.

6. Before World War II astrologers were predicting that Hitler would not invade Poland.[37] He did.

Not *one* astrologer predicted any of the following events:

Recent airline crashes.

The stock-market crash of '87.

The Beijing massacre of Chinese students.

The Iranian hostage crisis.

The killing of over 200 Marines in Lebanon by a terrorist explosion.

The Mt. St. Helens explosion in Washington.

The San Francisco Bay/World Series Earthquake of '89.

Etc., etc., etc.

Can we trust astrology? No, but we can trust the Bible. Here is a guide for living, and a sure witness of events that have come to pass.

The stars witness of Jesus. The Bible tells us to "be not dismayed at the signs of heaven; for the heathen are dismayed at them" (Jeremiah 10:2).

# Reincarnation: The Wheel of Rebirth

The belief in reincarnation, also called "the transmigration of souls," is an old belief, found in all parts of the world. In 1969 the Gallup organization did an extensive ten-nation poll to rate the percentage of people who believe in reincarnation. Here are their findings:

| | |
|---|---|
| Austria: 20% | Netherlands: 10% |
| Canada: 26% | Norway: 14% |
| France: 23% | Sweden: 12% |
| Britain: 18% | United States: 20% |
| Greece: 22% | West Germany: 25% |

As the years have progressed, so have the percentages of people who believe in reincarnation. A new Gallup poll was taken in Great Britain in 1979. While 18 percent of the British believed in reincarnation in 1969, 23 percent of the men and 33 percent of the women professed a belief in it in 1979.[1]

The Gallup organization did a book in 1982 entitled *Adventures in Immortality*. The book was based on extensive polls done in the United States throughout 1981. One of the questions asked was, "Do you believe in reincarnation—that is the rebirth of the soul in a new body after death—or not?"

About one out of four, 23 percent, said they did. This included 21 percent of those calling themselves Baptist, 22 percent of those calling themselves Lutherans, and 26 percent of those calling themselves Methodists. Among Catholics the figure was 25 percent.[2]

Among college students in 1977, the percentage of reincarnation believers was at 31.[3]

The belief in reincarnation, which is foundational in Eastern religions, was first made popular in the West by Helena Petrovna Blavatsky, the founder of the Theosophical Society. Professor Carl Jackson, in his article in the current *Encyclopedia Britannica,* writes of Madame Blavatsky and her work:

> Theosophy is a religious philosophy with definite mystical concerns that can be traced to the ancient world but is of catalytic significance in religious thought in the 19th and 20th centuries . . . The movement has been a catalytic force in the 20th century revival of Buddhism and Hinduism, and a pioneering agency in the promotion of greater Western acquaintance with Eastern thought. In the United States it has influenced a whole series of religious movements . . . In the estimation of some scholars, no other single organization has done more to popularize Asian religions and philosophical ideas in the West.[4]

Madame Blavatsky obviously had a distinct hatred for Judeo-Christianity and the God worshipped by its adherents:

> The appellation Sa'tan, in Hebrew *Satan,* and Adversary . . . belongs by right to the first and cruelest "Adversary" of all other Gods—Jehovah; not to the serpent which spoke only words of sympathy and wisdom.[5]

> Satan, the serpent of Genesis, is the real creator and benefactor, the father of spiritual mankind. For it is he . . . who opened the eyes . . . And he who was the first to whisper, "In the day ye eat thereof, ye shall be

as Elohim, knowing good and evil," [which] can only be regarded in the light of a savior.[6]

Madame Blavatsky considered Jehovah to be the true "Satan" (meaning "adversary"). She considered the God of the Bible to be "capricious and unjust,"[7] plus "a tribal God and no more."[8] She said that Bible believers "are fighting against divine truth, when repudiating and slandering the Dragon of Esoteric Divine Wisdom."[9]

It still amazes me how reincarnationists will say that the Bible supports them, but once they have convinced the person of this doctrine they tell them either that the Bible has been altered or that it simply cannot be trusted.

## Reincarnation Vs. History

Again, reincarnation is an ancient belief. We hear about it first in the Garden of Eden. The Lord told Adam that he could eat of every tree of the garden, but not of "the tree of the knowledge of good and evil." If he did he would "surely die" (Genesis 2:17). The narrator continues with:

> Now the serpent was more subtil than any beast of the field which the LORD God had made. And he said unto the woman, Yea, hath God said, Ye shall not eat of every tree of the garden? And the woman said unto the serpent, We may eat of the fruit of the trees of the garden: But of the fruit of the tree which is in the midst of the garden, God hath said, Ye shall not eat of it, neither shall ye touch it, lest ye die. And the serpent said unto the woman, Ye shall not surely die (Genesis 3:1-4).

### No death

Before Adam and Eve partook of the forbidden fruit they lived in a world that did not know death or sin. Satan, who is Lucifer, lied to Eve by saying they would not die. They did. The teaching that there is "no death" is the foundation of reincarnation. Here are comments from a few reincarnationists:

### Jane Roberts

There is no separate, specific point of death. Life is a state of becoming, and death is a part of this process of becoming.[10]

### Elizabeth Kubler-Ross

Death is the final stage of growth in this life. There is no total death.[11]

### The Serpent

Ye shall not surely die (Genesis 3:4).

## Early beliefs

Many reincarnationists declare that reincarnation was originally a Christian doctrine, but was suppressed in later centuries by unenlightened church leaders and councils:

### L. P. Weatherhead

Christians should not be opposed to reincarnation because it was the original belief of the Jews, the Essenes, and the early church.[12]

Did the Jews believe in reincarnation? Leslie Weatherhead declares that Christianity actually came from the sect of the Essenes. He says that the Essenes "definitely taught it. And Josephus makes reference to it as if it were commonly accepted."[13] Weatherhead refers to Josephus's *Jewish Wars*. Yet, he doesn't quote that Jewish historian; he just refers to him saying that reincarnation was believed by the Essenes, and hence, commonly held. Let us see what Josephus really has to say:

[It is said that] on one hand souls are immortal, but on the other hand those of good men only are changed into another body, but those of evil men are subject to eternal punishment.[14]

Mr. Weatherhead just referred to it; he did not quote it. Now we see why. Does Josephus say here that the Essenes believe in reincarnation? No, he says they believed that good men would be "changed into another body" while evil men would be punished eternally. Reincarnationists believe that *all* of us, good or evil, will come back in another body. Also, reincarnationists *do not* believe in eternal punishment, since every soul eventually leaves the Wheel of Rebirth and enters Nirvana.

The Essenes probably believed that God would resurrect the good, and send the bad souls to Hell forever. The resurrection body, since it would be incorruptible, would indeed be a "different body" from the one we have now. Yet, we will still be who we are. Our personality and identity will not change, but the body will.

Even if the Essenes had believed in reincarnation (which they didn't) there is *no evidence* that Jesus had been an Essene. In fact, there is a lot of evidence indicating He could not have been. The sect of the Essenes were not to visit the Temple in Jerusalem, nor to eat or socialize with people outside their community. Jesus visited the Temple often, and ate with publicans and sinners! Very un-Essene behavior!

Did the early Christian church teach reincarnation? Christian researchers Joseph P Grudel, Robert M. Bowman, Jr., and Dan R. Schlesinger of the Christian Research Institute (a cult-watching organization based in Southern California), wrote a paper entitled "Reincarnation—Did the Church Suppress It?"[15] In it they exposed outright fabrications and deception on the part of some reincarnationists who were insisting the early church taught reincarnation but it was later suppressed.

One favorite ploy of the reincarnationists is to quote the early church father Origen (c. 185-245), saying he believed in reincarnation. The Christian researchers comment:

> Origen was admittedly one of the most brilliant and innovative theologians of the early church. He was also, however, infamous for his theological speculations. He is the church father most often cited by reincarnationists as teaching their doctrine. One passage frequently cited is the following, from Origen's *Against Celcus* (I.32), exactly as cited by reincarnationists Head and Cranston:
>
> > "Or is it not more in conformity with reason that every soul, for certain mysterious reasons (I speak now according to the opinion of Pythagoras, and Plato, and Empedocles, whom Celcus frequently names), is introduced into a body, and introduced according to its deserts and former actions? It is probable, therefore, that this soul also, which conferred more benefit by its [former] residence in the flesh than that of many men (to avoid prejudice, I do not say 'all'), stood in need of a body not only superior to others, but invested with all excellent qualities."
>
> Several comments regarding this passage need to be made. First, Origen qualifies his statement by saying, "I speak now according to the opinion of Pythagorus, and Plato, and Empedocles, whom Celsus frequently names." This qualification indicates that Origen is arguing on the basis of Celsus's beliefs, not Origen's own beliefs. One reincarnationist, Anthony J. Fisichella, omitted this entire clause when quoting the passage.[16]

The researchers go on to show how reincarnationists took out and added phrases to make Origen say something he didn't say. They took away the phrase "I speak now according to [pagan belief]" and added "former" in between "benefit by its" and "residence in the flesh." This is deliberate fabrication and deception! Origen was saying, "Now, you pagans believe such and such" and then compares their belief with his.

Indeed reincarnationists must have pored through Origen's writings to find (and misquote) this passage. Origen also wrote a commentary on the Gospel of Matthew in which he answered the question, Was John the Baptist the reincarnation of Elijah? Origen wrote:

> In this place (Matthew 17:10-13) it does not appear to me that by Elijah the soul is spoken of, lest I should fall into the dogma of transmigration, which is foreign to the church of God, and not handed down by the Apostles, nor anywhere set forth in the Scriptures.[17]

Origen was saying that reincarnation was (1) *foreign* to the church of God; (2) *not* handed down by the Apostles; and (3) *not anywhere* set forth in the Scriptures (the Bible). Origen's *Commentary on Matthew* has always been printed right alongside his other works, including the one the reincarnationists quote from. How could they have overlooked it? You know the answer.

## Reincarnation Vs. the Bible

In order to convert the West to the New Age, reincarnationists declare that the Judeo-Christian Scripture, the Bible, teaches reincarnation. Let's examine some of their claims.

### Jesus

For our purposes we'll reply to an article by New Age "Prophet" Benjamin Creme. He entitled his article "Reincarnation and Karma in the Bible." He writes:

> Generally speaking, people are unaware that there are definite references in the New Testament that unequivocally imply reincarnation.[18]

> The first sign [for reincarnation] is found in Matthew 11:13,14; 16:13. Jesus is asking His disciples, "Whom do men say that I, the son of man, am?" (Matthew 16:13) and the disciples answer, "Some say that

thou art John the Baptist, some Elias and others Jeremias, or one of the prophets." How could Jesus be thought to be any of these except in a past life?[19]

THE BIBLE

In truth, the people could *not* have meant reincarnation, because John the Baptist had *just been killed!* Reincarnation does not mean coming back immediately as a full-grown man! However, the Jews did believe in the resurrection of the dead. Many thought Jesus was actually the resurrected (*not* reincarnated) John the Baptist, or some other prophet. He was not. Who was He? Let's see:

> He saith unto them, But whom say ye that I am?
>
> And Simon Peter answered and said, Thou art the Christ, the Son of the living God.
>
> And Jesus answered and said unto him, Blessed art thou, Simon Bar-jona: for flesh and blood hath not revealed it unto thee, but my Father which is in heaven (Matthew 16:15,17).

## John the Baptist

### Benjamin Creme

Jesus himself tells his disciples who John the Baptist was in the past: "For all prophets and the law prophesied until John. And if ye will receive it, this is Elias, which was for to come. He that hath ears to hear let him hear" (Matthew 11:13-15). So, Elias, according to Jesus himself, came back to earth in the personality of John the Baptist.[20]

### The Bible

According to the Word of God, the Bible, Elijah the prophet was taken to God without tasting death (2 Kings 2:11). According to the Lord through his prophet Malachi, Elijah would be sent "before the coming of the great and dreadful day of the LORD" (Malachi 4:5). The people expected the appearance of the prophet Elijah before the appearance of the Messiah. John the Baptist did indeed come with "the spirit and power" of Elijah. This does not mean that Elijah had reincarnated as John. We know this because Elijah actually appeared on the Mount of Transfiguration soon after John was beheaded:

> And after six days Jesus taketh Peter, James, and John his brother, and bringeth them up into an high mountain apart, and was transfigured before them: and his face did shine as the sun, and his raiment was white as the light. And behold, there appeared unto them Moses and Elias talking with him (Matthew 17:1-3).

This presents a couple of serious problems for reincarnationists. When you reincarnate you are supposed to (1) lose all memory of your former incarnations, and (2) be a new personality. So first, who did Elijah reincarnate as? It couldn't have been John the Baptist. Second, Moses was there—who did he reincarnate as? Third, it may be argued that Moses and Elias (the Greek name for Elijah) were ghosts. Yet reincarnationists believe that Jesus was a reincarnation of Moses. How can a disembodied entity, or spirit, talk to itself in another living body with three mortal onlookers standing by? Very strange indeed!

How do we take it when the Bible says that John the Baptist was "in the spirit and power of Elias" (Luke 1:17)? First, if this implies reincarnation, it would have said that "the spirit of Elias was in John," not that John was sent "in the spirit and power of Elias." Let's assume that what Luke is saying implies reincarnation. Okay, according to Luke 1:17, John the Baptist (body and soul) was literally "in" not only the "spirit" but also the "power" of Elijah. But wait! This doesn't make any sense. How can a living man, made up of body and soul, be "in" his own reincarnated spirit and "in" something called that entity's "power"? This doesn't work! What does? We often speak of the "spirit" of patriotism, or around Christmas time being "in" a "joyful spirit." Obviously, we cannot enter any spirit (non-material being).

It makes sense that what the Bible is talking about is this: John the Baptist came in the "spirit and power of Elijah." John came to do the things Elijah would have done. John came "in the attitude" of Elijah. He came in the "power" or with the same God-given authority as Elijah. If God would send a prophet "like unto" Moses (Deuteronomy 18:15,18) to be His Messiah, but who was not literally Moses, then in like manner, He could send a prophet like unto Elijah who was not literally Elijah.

It is ironic how New Age propagandists take literal passages of the Bible and call them symbolic, while taking symbolic passages and calling them literal. John came "in the spirit and power" of Elijah, meaning he came to fulfill Elijah's office as forerunner to the Messiah. Therefore, reincarnation is not taught here since (1) Elijah never died (2 Kings 2:11); (2) Elijah appeared on the Mount of Transfiguration (Matthew 17:1-3); and (3) when asked, "Are you Elijah?" John replied, "I am not" (John 1:21).

## The blind man

*Benjamin Creme*

The third reference comes as a question concerning a blind man. The disciples ask Jesus, "Who did sin, this man, or his parents, that he was born blind?" (John 9:2). How could a man sin before he was born unless the sin was committed in another life?[21]

THE BIBLE

This would have been a golden opportunity for Jesus to teach reincarnation and Karma. Under those beliefs, if you were born, let's say, blind, then it *must* be the result of sins in a previous life. Your parents were, under the law of Karma, also being punished. All suffering, without exception, is the result of Karma (the debt a soul collects by wrong deeds). Suffering seeks to burn away the Karma as an incinerator seeks to burn waste, or, perhaps, as the body burns with fever in order to fight an infection.

The disciples of Jesus ask an odd question: "Which is it, Master? Did this man sin, or was it his parents' sins?" If Jesus was teaching reincarnation, He wasn't doing a very good job. Under the Law of Karma both the blind man *and* his parents were being punished for previous misdeeds.

This is not an either/or situation. To ask which one sinned would be like pointing to a lamp and asking, Which makes it light, the electricity or the bulb? Well, without the electricity there would be no light. Without the bulb the electricity is useless, and, again, there would be no light. No, there must be another explanation.

According to the Law of Karma, all suffering is necessary so a soul can progress in its cosmic evolution. To relieve suffering (like healing a blind man) in this life would only cause the soul to become blind for that much longer in future incarnations. Also, his parents probably would have another blind child because they would still need to suffer as well. The Law of Karma says suffering should not be relieved but accepted as beneficial and absolutely necessary to the soul. Jesus violated this "inviolate" law when He healed the blind man. A very strange thing to do for someone who supposedly taught reincarnation and Karma.

The question arises, What did the disciples mean by their odd question? We must not forget that Jesus lived during the time the Romans occupied the Holy Land. With them came pagan ideas, as well as pagan traders, soldiers, merchants, officials, artisans, sailors and colonists. They believed in reincarnation and Karma. Wherever Jesus went, great crowds followed Him. When He came to the blind man one can almost hear some of the crowd saying, "Look here, in a previous life this man must have sinned, and that's why he was born blind."

The more orthodox among them would have taken offense at this and would have said something like, "No, his parents must have done some horrible sin before the man was born, and God is punishing them through him."

The disciples, hearing the crowd, asked the Master, "Which is it, Master? Which is right? Did this man sin, or was it his parents?"

If Jesus believed in reincarnation and Karma then His *only choice* for an answer would be: "Both are correct. Both the man and his parents are being punished for their sins." Yet, Jesus' answer was:

> Neither hath this man sinned, nor his parents: but that the works of God should be made manifest in him (John 9:3).

Jesus then *violated* the so-called sacred and inviolate Law of Karma by healing the man.

## The truth

The gospels were meant to be missionary tracts to convert the world, which, at that time, was primarily pagan. The chief doctrines of paganism are reincarnation and Karma. These verses which Creme and other Aquarian ministers and missionaries use as "proof" that Jesus taught reincarnation and Karma are actually profound and unequivocal denunciations of both!

As astrology is a corruption of Mazzaroth, so are reincarnation and Karma a corruption of the truth. Reincarnation teaches that we have souls, and these souls pass through many lives on earth. In truth, we do have souls, but our lifetime on earth is just once (Hebrews 9:27).

Karma teaches that our misdeeds work up a spiritual debt, and that suffering repays it. In truth, our sins do indeed work up a spiritual debt, but the sentence we receive for it is eternity in Hell without the possibility of parole. Only by accepting Jesus as our Lord and Savior can we avert the unspeakable fate that awaits us.

The blood of Jesus is not a parole; it is a full pardon. The apostle John wrote:

> For God so loved the world that he gave his only begotten Son, that whosoever believeth in him should not perish, but have everlasting life. For God sent not his Son into the world to condemn the world; but that the world through him might be saved (John 3:16,17).

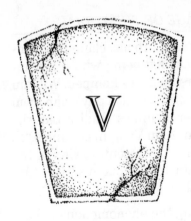

# Channeling: Is It From God?

In recent years mediumship has arisen to great heights of popularity. What is mediumship? It is when a person, claiming to be a psychic or clairvoyant, purports to offer himself or herself as a channel between the spirit world and our material world. A medium operates as a "go-between."

A hundred years ago mediums concentrated on conjuring up the dead relatives or perhaps the favorite author or celebrity of the aspirant seeker who footed the bill for the seers' services. Nowadays mediums call themselves "channelers." The spirits, or entities as the mediums like to call them, which they conjure up are more apt to be someone like a 35,000-year-old warrior-king from Lemuria rather than, let's say, a rich dead aunt who never left a will.

Who are some of the most celebrated "channelers" of today? J. Z. Knight is probably the most well known. She purports to channel Ramtha, the 35,000-year-old warrior-king mentioned above. Jach Pursel channels "Lazaris" (not to be confused with Lazarus, the man Jesus raised from the dead), a being who reports that he has never entered the material realm by an incarnation. Kevin Ryerson claims to channel a good number of different entities. Penny Torres, a former Catholic, claims to channel "Mafu," a seventh-dimensional being whose last incarnation was as a leper in first-century Pompeii. William Rainan channels "Dr. Peebles," a Scottish physician from the 19th century. Verna Yater channels "Indira Latari," a 19th-century Indian woman. Alan Vaughn channels "Li Sung," a village philosopher from 8th-century China. Iris Belhayes channels "Enid," an Irish woman of the 19th century. The list goes on and on.

I noticed, while studying the phenomenon of channeling, that virtually all the channelers began their careers after they personally witnessed one or more ghostly manifestations. This manifestation, or apparition if you will, would always tell the person that he or she had been chosen to deliver an important message to mankind. These apparitions were always triggered by the channelers initially working on a Ouija Board.

## The Ouija Board

In 1853 a French spiritist, an M. Planchett, reinvented an ancient device now known as the Ouija Board. Planchett's device consisted of a small heart-shaped, table-like board with three legs, one of which was a pencil. The operator, called the "sitter," placed his fingers on top of the device and lightly held them there as it moved across a piece of paper. It was hoped that a message from the spirit would appear on the paper. This device became popularly known among spiritists as a "Planchett."

In 1889 an American by the name of William Fuld recreated the "Planchett," this time using an alphabet table instead of a pencil and a piece of paper. He renamed the Planchett "Ouija," *oui* meaning yes in French and *ja* meaning yes in German.

In 1914, the respected American Society for Psychical Research made a study of the Ouija Board. In one test they blindfolded the sitter, covered the surface of the board, and then secretly rearranged the alphabet on the board. The sitter "channeled" a message with unusual speed and accuracy. The director of the experiment, Sir William F. Barrett, concluded:

> Reviewing the results as a whole, I am convinced of their supernormal character, and that we have here an exhibition of some intelligent, disincarnate agency, mingling with the personality of one or more of the sitters and guiding their muscular movements.[1]

The board became very popular up to and during the 1920s, selling in the millions. In 1966 the rights to the board were sold to Parker Brothers of (you'll never believe) Salem, Massachusetts.

## Strange goings-on

During the '70s the Ouija Board grew even more popular. Then things began to happen. Reports were coming in from all over the country about strange and horrifying occurrences related to the use of the board. At first the stories only increased the sales of the board. Yet, as time went on, the stories became more frequent and more terrifying. There were so many stories, true and false, that sales began to drop dramatically. It was during the mid '70s that many of our present-day channelers experimented with the board.

A number of individuals, both pro- and anti-New Age, made studies of some of those cases in which paranormal activity with the board was claimed. Here are a few comments from these researchers:

*Nandor Fodor, Psychic Researcher*

> Many researchers have pointed out the inherent dangers of using the Ouija Board or of taking the "messages" seriously, because of the possibility of dredging

up some very unpleasant and potentially disturbing attitudes and facts from one's subconscious. There have been numerous instances of persons who have become very upset emotionally from the use of the Ouija Board.[2]

### Carl Wickland, M.D., Psychiatrist

The serious problem of alienation and mental derangement attending ignorant psychic experiments was first brought to my attention by cases of several persons whose seemingly harmless experience with automatic writing and the Ouija Board resulted in such wild insanity that commitment to asylums was necessitated . . . Many other disastrous results which followed the use of the supposedly innocent Ouija Board came to my notice, and my observation led me into research in psychic phenomena for a possible explanation of these strange occurrences.[3]

### G. Godfrey Raupert, Investigator

Suggestions are made in the most subtle manner, in exalted language, appealing to the youthful imagination and to dangerous tendencies latent in all men; and when it is borne in mind that the invisible counselor who makes these suggestions is believed to be a kindly father or mother who could only desire the well-being of her child, and that the experimenter's power of discrimination is lost, one can imagine how far this kind of mischief can be carried.

As the "psychic development" advances, the entire mental and moral nature of the experimenter becomes disordered; and he discovers to his cost that, while it was an easy thing for him to *open* the mental door by which the mind could be invaded, it is a difficult, if not an impossible thing, to *shut* that door and to expel the invader. For the impulse to communicate or to write now asserts itself imperatively and incessantly, at all hours of the day and in the midst of every kind of occupation and, in the end, even at night, either suddenly awakening the victim or preventing him from securing any refreshing sleep. A pitiable condition of mental and moral collapse, often terminating in suicide or insanity, is frequently the ultimate result.[4]

*Pastor H. R. Neff, Minister and Researcher*

A sufficient number of people have gotten into serious psychological difficulty through use of a Ouija Board to warn us that these instruments may not be "innocent toys." Most serious students of parapsychology strongly advise people not to use Ouija Boards and such instruments.[5]

What good can come from this "bad fruit"? The channelers want you to believe that the entities they channel are wise and benevolent beings from long ago who want only what is good for humanity. They claim that Jesus was an Ascended Master Himself, and that the Bible is just ancient channeled messages which are true, but out-dated.

## Channeling and Christ

Let's take a few of these channeled messages, and compare them with the Bible. If the Bible once was a "channeled" message from the same group of beings, it might be out-dated, but it would not contradict present-day channeled material.

Jane Roberts is famous for channeling "Seth." She met "Seth" one day while working a Ouija Board. In one of her books, after more than 6,000 pages of messages, "Seth" declares:

Christ, the historical Christ, was not crucified . . . He had no intention of dying in that manner; but others felt that to fulfill the prophecies in all ways, a crucifixion was a necessity.

Christ did not take part in it. There was a conspiracy in which Judas played a role, an attempt to make a martyr out of Christ. The man chosen was drugged—hence the necessity of helping him carry the cross (see Luke 23)—and he was told that he was the Christ.

He believed that he was . . . the tomb was empty because this same group carted the body away . . . Peter three times denied the Lord (Matthew 26), saying he did not know Him, because he recognized that that person was not Christ.[6]

After "Seth" has flattered you, and astounded you with his amazing insight into human nature, he tells you, "Christ was never crucified"! Not only does he tell you that Christ was never crucified, but "Seth" also quotes the Bible to "prove" it! Let's briefly analyze the revelations of "Seth":

SETH: The historical Christ was not crucified.

COMMENT

The biblical Christ was crucified. If the biblical Christ is the historical Christ, the Bible is inaccurate as an historical record. If the Bible is untrustworthy, why does "Seth" quote from it to prove his point? The Bible, in fact, is accurate. The Bible says that Jesus was crucified (Matthew 27:35).

SETH: Jesus had no intention of dying in that manner; but others felt that to fulfill the prophecies in all ways, a crucifixion was a necessity.

COMMENT

The Bible says just the opposite: It says Jesus knew He had to be crucified, and He would not let His disciples try to persuade Him otherwise:

And he began to teach them, that the Son of man must suffer many things, and be rejected of the elders, and of the chief priests, and scribes, and be killed, and after three days rise again. And he spake that saying openly. And Peter took him, and began to rebuke him. But when he had turned about and looked on his disciples, he rebuked Peter, saying, Get thee behind me, Satan: for thou savourest not the things that be of God, but the things that be of men (Mark 8:31-33).

SETH: Christ did not take part in it. The man crucified was drugged—that's why he needed help to carry the cross (see Luke 23).

## COMMENT

Okay, let's look at Luke 23. This chapter identifies Jesus with Christ (vss. 8, 26, 28, etc.). The man who carried the cross for Jesus was Simon of Cyrene (v. 26). Who was crucified? Let's see:

And when Jesus had cried with a loud voice, he said, Father, into thy hands I commend my spirit; and having said thus, he gave up the ghost (Luke 23:46).

According to Luke 23, Jesus was crucified—no drugging, no substitute "Christ," no kidding!

SETH: The tomb was empty because this same group carted the body away.

## COMMENT

According to all four gospel accounts, on the first day of the week the women found the tomb empty. They ran and told the disciples, and the disciples came and found it empty. Jesus appeared to Mary, then to two disciples on the road, and to the eleven later. The Bible also says that angels appeared, and that the chief priests gave the soldiers large sums of money to say Jesus' disciples had stolen His body at night (Matthew 28).

SETH: Peter three times denied the Lord (Matthew 26), saying he did not know Him, because he recognized that that person was not Christ.

## COMMENT

The Bible says differently:

And the Lord said, Simon, Simon, behold, Satan hath
desired to have you, that he may sift you as wheat: but
I have prayed for thee, that thy faith fail not: and when
thou art converted, strengthen thy brethren.

And he said unto him, Lord, I am ready to go with thee,
both into prison, and to death.

And he said, I tell thee, Peter, the cock shall not crow
this day, before that thou shalt thrice deny that thou
knowest me (Luke 22:31-34).

In a temporary moment of faithlessness, and perhaps a measure of cowardice, Peter denied knowing Jesus, being a disciple of His, and even being from Galilee.
The Bible says it was Jesus Himself whom Peter denied.

As we have seen, "Seth" quoted the Bible to prove
a point. Yet, the Bible itself totally refutes the point that
"Seth" was trying to make. The entity called "Seth" has
neither been honest nor logically consistent. Shall we
trust "Seth," or any other conjured-up entity, with our
eternal souls? Think about it.

By far the most famous channeler these days is J.
Z. Knight. She channels "Ramtha." Here is a brief extract
from a conversation between Ramtha (being channeled
by Knight) and a disciple:

DISCIPLE: My main concern is what my path of service is in my life.

RAMTHA: To you.

DISCIPLE: To myself and my fellow man.

RAMTHA: Don't worry about your fellow man. If you
become happy, however others look upon you doesn't
make any difference. The fact that you are happy and
in service to Self is quite enough.[7]

Ramtha says not to worry about our fellow man,
but to worship Self. Jesus taught the opposite:

DISCIPLE: Master, which is the great commandment

of the law?

JESUS: Thou shalt love the Lord thy God with all thy heart, and with all thy soul, and with all thy mind. This is the first great commandment. And the second is like unto it, Thou shalt love thy neighbour as thyself (Matthew 22:36-39).

Jesus also said:

Whosoever will save his life shall lose it: and whosoever will lose his life for my sake shall find it (Matthew 16:25).

## Channeling Vs. the Bible

The Bible condemns the occultic practice of channeling in no uncertain terms:

Regard not them that have familiar spirits, neither seek after wizards, to be defiled by them: I am the LORD your God (Leviticus 19:31).

And the soul that turneth after such as have familiar spirits, and after wizards, to go awhoring after them, I will even set my face against that soul, and will cut him off from among his people (Leviticus 20:6).

When thou art come into the land which the LORD thy God giveth thee, thou shalt not learn to do after the abominations of those nations. There shall not be found among you any one that maketh his son or his daughter to pass through the fire, or that useth divination, or any observer of times, or an enchanter, or a witch, Or a charmer, or a consulter with familiar spirits, or a wizard, or a necromancer (Deuteronomy 18:9-11).

In case you don't know, a necromancer is one who communicates with the spirit world. Today we would call him a channeler. Many other Scriptures condemn channeling, including: 1 Samuel 28:3; 2 Kings 21:6; 23:24; 1 Chronicles 10:13; 2 Chronicles 33:6; Isaiah 8:19; 19:3; Acts 19:11-17.

The evil entities that the Bible calls "familiar spirits" cannot be trusted. They seek only the destruction of humanity. Only the power of Jesus can free the soul from their destructive influences.

# Prophecy:
# True
# or False?

As we saw in the previous chapter, God warns us through His Holy Word against necromancers (channelers), star-gazers (astrologers) and false prophets. We have seen how astrology is unbiblical and unscientific. Don't let it get into your head for a minute, though, that the occultic arts are just illusions or fabrications.

The author of these occultic practices and beliefs is Lucifer, and he does indeed have power and knowledge which far surpasses that of man. Yet, God's power and wisdom is infinitely greater than Satan's. The evil entity we call Lucifer has been a keen student of world events and human nature for at least the last six thousand years. He also has a lot to do with how this world is actually run. That's a pretty tough combination to beat! Satan has untold myriads of "familiar spirits" that enforce his decrees around the world. It shouldn't surprise us that he can predict events on occasion. It is more astonishing, though, to view his track record and see how many mistakes he makes, given his superior intellect and the fact that he is "the god of this world" (2 Corinthians 4:4).

Lucifer fell because he wanted to replace God with his own candidate for the job—himself (Isaiah 14). Wanting to be the Most High and being Him are two different things. Lucifer wishes to imitate God by appointing his own prophets, and channeling his own bibles. Yet, these will not benefit humanity. Lucifer hates God—and His creation. He seeks to destroy it.

You may now be asking: "How can such an intelligent being be so evil and destructive?"

Was not Hitler an evil genius? Was he not destructive, even after he *knew* for a certainty the doom of his cause? The same is true for Lucifer. He seeks not to save, but to *destroy*.

## Jeane Dixon's Prophecies

Perhaps the best known psychic of the 20th century is Jeane Dixon. Many of her prophecies have been quite accurate. Here are a few examples:

1. In 1952 she prophesied that a Democrat would become President in 1960, and that he would be assassinated while in office.

COMMENT: President Kennedy, a Democrat, was assassinated while in office in 1963.

2. In 1945 she prophesied that President Roosevelt would die within six months.

COMMENT: Four months later President Roosevelt died of a cerebral hemorrhage.

3. Though political experts disagreed with her, in 1946 she prophesied that China would soon be Communist.

COMMENT: She proved the experts wrong. China became Communist in 1948.

4. In 1946 she prophesied that India would be free, but partitioned, within two years.

COMMENT: In 1947 India was free, but was partitioned into India and Pakistan.

5. In 1947 she prophesied that Gandhi would be assassinated within six months.

COMMENT: Six months later Gandhi lay dead from assassins' bullets.

Here is a partial list of additional prophecies by Dixon that have come to pass:

Truman's re-election

Merging of the AFL-CIO

Re-election of Eisenhower

Death of Secretary of State John Dulles

Plane crash of Dag Hammarskjold

Prayer banning in public schools

Death of Sir Winston Churchill

Plane crash of Senator Edward Kennedy

Assassination of Robert Kennedy

Election of Richard Nixon as President

Assassination of Martin Luther King, Jr.

One might say that these were good guesses, but this doesn't work. For example, one might "guess" that Martin Luther King, Jr., would be assassinated. Yet, Dixon said he would be killed by an assassin's bullet in the neck. This is exactly what happened. There are many more cases such as this.[1]

Along with true prophecies, however, Dixon has had an equally long string of false prophecies. Here is a partial list of those that have *not* come to pass:

1. She prophesied that President Eisenhower

would appoint Gen. Douglas MacArthur to a high post in his administration.

COMMENT: This never happened.

2. In 1953 she prophesied that two American generals would soon help defeat the Communists in China.

COMMENT: The Communists defeated the Chinese Nationalists — and their American advisors.

3. She prophesied that Russia would invade Iran in 1953, and Palestine in 1957.

COMMENT: Neither occurred.

4. She prophesied that World War III would break out in 1958.

COMMENT: 1958 was an unusually peaceful year.

5. She prophesied, once she saw that the Red Chinese would not be defeated, that Red China would be admitted into the United Nations in 1959.

COMMENT: They were not admitted until many years later.

Here are more failed prophecies of Dixon:

China and Russia would be one country in 1964.

The Vietnam War would end by September of 1966.

In 1957 Congress would appoint an "Assistant

President" (between the President and the Vice President).

Castro would die in 1966.

Russia would land a man on the moon first.

Track records of other prominent, and not so prominent, psychics are similar to Jeane Dixon's.[2]

Aquarians follow these psychics because they are amazed at their prophetic abilities. What about when the psychics miss? Well, the Aquarian either goes to a new psychic, or explains it away by saying that the psychic "had bad cosmic vibrations" that day, etc.

THE BIBLE

The Lord said, through His prophet Moses:

> When a prophet speaketh in the name of the LORD, if the thing follow not, nor come to pass, that is the thing which the LORD hath not spoken, but the prophet hath spoken it presumptuously: thou shalt not be afraid of him (Deuteronomy 18:22).

Be assured that the psychic has power, but does that necessarily mean that this power is good? Be assured also that the God of the Bible is *not* the author of the psychic's messages! Will you trust your eternal soul to a being who is, at best, hit-or-miss, or to a Being who is your Creator, and who loves you? The choice is yours. Aquarian prophecy cannot be trusted, but the Bible can.

Here are some of the most important prophecies of the Bible, and how they were fulfilled in Jesus, the one and only Christ.

## Bible Prophecies and Their Fulfillment

● The Messiah would be born of the seed of a woman, not of the seed of a man:

*Prophecy*

And I will put enmity between thee and the woman, and between thy seed and her seed; it shall bruise thy head, and thou shalt bruise his heel (Genesis 3:15).

*Fulfillment*

But when the fulness of the time was come, God sent forth his Son, made of a woman, made under the law (Galatians 4:4).

● The Messiah was to be born of a virgin:

*Prophecy*

Therefore the Lord himself shall give you a sign; Behold, a virgin shall conceive, and bear a son, and shall call his name Immanuel (Isaiah 7:14).

*Fulfillment*

And in the sixth month the angel Gabriel was sent from God unto a city of Galilee, named Nazareth, to a virgin espoused to a man whose name was Joseph, of the house of David; and the virgin's name was Mary . . . And the angel said unto her, Fear not, Mary: for thou hast found favor with God. And, behold, thou shalt conceive in thy womb, and bring forth a son, and shalt call his name JESUS (Luke 1:26,27,30,31).

● The Messiah would be called the Son of God:

*Prophecy*

I will declare the decree: the LORD hath said unto me, Thou art my Son; this day have I begotten thee (Psalm 2:7).

*Fulfillment*

And Jesus, when he was baptized, went up straightway out of the water: and, lo, the heavens were opened unto him, and he saw the Spirit of God descending like a dove, and lighting upon him: And lo a voice from heaven, saying, This is my beloved Son, in whom I am well pleased (Matthew 3:16,17).

● The Messiah was to be of the seed of Abraham:

*Prophecy*

And in thy seed shall all the nations of the earth be blessed; because thou hast obeyed my voice (Genesis 22:18).

*Fulfillment*

The book of the generation of Jesus Christ, the son of David, the son of Abraham (Matthew 1:1).

● A new star in the heavens would appear at the Messiah's birth:

*Prophecy*

I shall see him, but not now; I shall behold him, but not nigh; there shall come a Star out of Jacob, and a Scepter shall rise out of Israel, and shall smite the corners of Moab, and destroy the children of Shath (Numbers 24:17).

*Fulfillment*

Now when Jesus was born in Bethlehem of Judæa in the days of Herod the king, behold, there came wise men from the east to Jerusalem, saying, Where is he that is born King of the Jews? for we have seen his star in the east, and are come to worship him . . . When they had heard the king, they departed; and, lo, the star, which they saw in the east, went before them, till it came and stood over where the young child was (Matthew 2:1,2,9).

● The Messiah would be born of the tribe of Judah:

*Prophecy*

The sceptre shall not depart from Judah, nor a lawgiver from between his feet, until Shiloh come; and unto him shall the gathering of the people be (Genesis 49:10).

*Fulfillment*

Jesus . . . the son of Juda (Luke 3:23,33).

● The Messiah would be a descendant of Jesse:

*Prophecy*

And there shall come forth a rod out of the stem of Jesse, and a Branch shall grow out of his roots (Isaiah 11:1).

*Fulfillment*

Jesus . . . the son of Jesse (Luke 3:23,32).

● The Messiah would be of the royal House of David:

*Prophecy*

Behold, the days come, saith the LORD, that I will raise unto David a righteous Branch, and a King shall reign and prosper, and shall execute judgment and justice in the earth (Jeremiah 23:5).

*Fulfillment*

Jesus . . . the son of David (Luke 3:23,31).

● The Messiah would be born at Bethlehem:

*Prophecy*

But thou, Bethlehem Ephratah, though thou be little among the thousands of Judah, yet out of thee shall he come forth unto me that is to be ruler in Israel; whose goings forth have been from of old, from everlasting (Micah 5:2).

*Fulfillment*

Jesus was born in Bethlehem of Judæa (Matthew 2:1).

● When the Messiah was born, a wicked king would try to kill Him, and would kill many innocent children in that effort:

*Prophecy*

Thus saith the LORD: A voice was heard in Ramah, lamentation, and bitter weeping, Rahel weeping for her children refused to be comforted for her children, because they were not (Jeremiah 31:15).

*Fulfillment*

Then Herod, when he saw that he was mocked of the wise men, was exceeding wroth, and sent forth, and slew all the children that were in Bethlehem, and in all the coasts thereof, from two years old and under, according to the time which he had diligently enquired of the wise men (Matthew 2:16).

● The Messiah would be called the Lord:

*Prophecy*

The LORD said unto my Lord, Sit thou at my right hand, until I make thine enemies thy footstool (Psalm 110:1).

*Fulfillment*

For unto you is born this day in the city of David a Saviour, which is Christ the Lord (Luke 2:11).

● The Messiah would be the Great High Priest after the order of Melchizedek:

*Prophecy*

The LORD hath sworn, and will not repent, Thou art a priest for ever after the order of Melchizedek (Psalm 110:4).

*Fulfillment*

So also Christ glorified not himself to be made an high priest; but he that said unto him, Thou art my Son, to day have I begotten thee. As he saith also in another place, Thou art a priest for ever after the order of Melchisedec (Hebrews 5:5,6).

● The Spirit of God would rest on the Messiah in a special way:

*Prophecy*

And there shall come forth a rod out of the stem of Jesse, and a Branch shall grow out of his roots: And the spirit of the LORD shall rest upon him, the spirit of wisdom and understanding, the spirit of counsel and might, the spirit of knowledge and of the fear of the LORD (Isaiah 11:1,2).

*Fulfillment*

And Jesus, when he was baptized, went up straightway out of the water: and, lo, the heavens were opened unto him, and he saw the Spirit of God descending like a dove, and lighting upon him: And lo a voice from heaven, saying, This is my beloved Son, in whom I am well pleased (Matthew 3:16,17).

● The Messiah would be heralded by a great prophet:

*Prophecy*

The voice of him that crieth in the wilderness, Prepare ye the way of the LORD, make straight in the desert a highway for our God (Isaiah 40:3).

*Fulfillment*

In those days came John the Baptist, preaching in the wilderness of Judæa, And saying, Repent ye: for the kingdom of heaven is at hand (Matthew 3:1,2).

● The Messiah would begin His mortal ministry in Galilee:

*Prophecy*

Nevertheless the dimness shall not be such as was in her vexation, when at the first he lightly afflicted the land of Zebulun and the land of Naphtali, and afterward did more grievously afflict her by the way of the sea, beyond Jordan, in Galilee of the nations. The people that walked in darkness have seen a great light: they that dwell in the land of the shadow of death, upon them hath the light shined (Isaiah 9:1,2).

*Fulfillment*

Now when Jesus had heard that John was cast into prison, he departed into Galilee; and leaving Nazareth,

he came and dwelt in Capernaum, which is upon the
sea coast, in the borders of Zabulon and Nephthalim
... From that time Jesus began to preach, and to say,
Repent: for the kingdom of heaven is at hand (Matthew
4:12,13,17).

● The ministry of the Messiah would be one of
miracles:

*Prophecy*

Then the eyes of the blind shall be opened, and the ears
of the deaf shall be unstopped. Then shall the lame man
leap as an hart, and the tongue of the dumb sing (Isaiah
35:5,6).

*Fulfillment*

And Jesus went about all the cities and villages, teaching in their synagogues, and preaching the gospel of the
kingdom, and healing every sickness and every disease
among the people (Matthew 9:35).

● The Messiah would teach by example and in
parable:

*Prophecy*

I will open my mouth in a parable: I will utter dark
sayings of old (Psalm 78:2).

*Fulfillment*

All these things spake Jesus unto the multitude in
parables; and without a parable spake he not unto them
(Matthew 13:34).

● The Messiah would enter Jerusalem on a
donkey:

*Prophecy*

Rejoice greatly, O daughter of Zion, shout, O daughter
of Jerusalem: behold, thy King cometh unto thee: he is
just, and having salvation, lowly, and riding upon an
ass, and upon a colt the foal of an ass (Zechariah 9:9).

*Fulfillment*

And the disciples went, and did as Jesus commanded them, and brought the ass, and the colt, and put on them their clothes, and they set him thereon . . . And the multitudes that went before, and that followed, cried, saying, Hosanna to the Son of David: Blessed is he that cometh in the name of the Lord; Hosanna in the highest (Matthew 21:6,7,9).

● The Messiah would be a head stone of the corner for believers, but a stone of stumbling to the Jews:

*Prophecy*

I will praise thee: for thou hast heard me, and art become my salvation. The stone which the builders refused is become the head stone of the corner . . . And he shall be for a sanctuary; but for a stone of stumbling and for a rock of offence to both the houses of Israel (Psalm 118:21,22; Isaiah 8:14).

*Fulfillment*

Unto you therefore which believe he is precious: but unto them which be disobedient, the stone which the builders disallowed, the same is made the head of the corner, And a stone of stumbling, and a rock of offence, even to them which stumble at the word (1 Peter 2:7,8).

● The Messiah would be betrayed by a friend:

*Prophecy*

Yea, mine own familiar friend, in whom I trusted, which did eat of my bread, hath lifted up his heel against me (Psalm 41:9).

*Fulfillment*

Judas Iscariot, who also betrayed him (Matthew 10:4).

● The betrayer of the Messiah would be given thirty pieces of silver:

*Prophecy*

And I said unto them, If ye think good, give me my price; and if not, forbear. So they weighed for my price thirty pieces of silver. And the LORD said unto me, Cast it unto the potter: a goodly price that I was prised at of them. And I took the thirty pieces of silver, and cast them to the potter in the house of the LORD (Zechariah 11:12,13).

*Fulfillment*

Then one of the twelve, called Judas Iscariot, went unto the chief priests, and said unto them, What will ye give me, and I will deliver him unto you? And they covenanted with him for thirty pieces of silver . . . And he cast down the pieces of silver in the temple, and departed . . . And they took counsel, and bought with them the potter's field, to bury strangers in (Matthew 26:14,15; 27:5,7).

● The Messiah would be forsaken by His disciples:

*Prophecy*

Awake, O sword, against my shepherd, and against the man that is my fellow, saith the LORD of hosts: smite the shepherd, and the sheep shall be scattered: and I will turn mine hand upon the little ones (Zechariah 13:7).

*Fulfillment*

Then saith Jesus unto them, All ye shall be offended because of me this night: for it is written, I will smite the shepherd, and the sheep of the flock shall be scattered abroad . . . and they all forsook him, and fled (Matthew 26:31; Mark 14:50).

● The Messiah would be dumb before His accusers:

*Prophecy*

He was oppressed, and he was afflicted, yet he opened not his mouth: he is brought as a lamb to the slaughter, and as a sheep before her shearers is dumb, so he openeth not his mouth (Isaiah 53:7).

*Fulfillment*

And when he was accused of the chief priests and elders, he answered nothing (Matthew 27:12).

● The Messiah would be smitten and spat upon:

*Prophecy*

I gave my back to the smiters, and my cheeks to them that plucked off the hair: I hid not my face from shame and spitting (Isaiah 50:6).

*Fulfillment*

Then did they spit in his face, and buffeted him, and others smote him with the palms of their hands (Matthew 26:67).

● The Messiah would be pierced to atone for sin:

*Prophecy*

For dogs have compassed me: the assembly of the wicked have inclosed me: they pierced my hands and my feet (Psalm 22:16).

But he was wounded for our transgressions, he was bruised for our iniquities; the chastisement of our peace was upon him; and with his stripes we are healed (Isaiah 53:5).

*Fulfillment*

Then delivered he him therefore unto them to be crucified. And they took Jesus, and led him away (John 19:16).

● The Messiah would be crucified with thieves:

*Prophecy*

Because he hath poured out his soul unto death: and he was numbered with the transgressors; and he bare the sin of many, and made intercession for the transgressors . . . (Isaiah 53:12).

*Fulfillment*

Then were there two thieves crucified with him, one on the right hand, and another on the left (Matthew 27:38).

● Those who followed the Messiah would stand afar off, while those who rejected Him would wag their heads:

*Prophecy*

My lovers and my friends stand aloof from my sore; and my kinsmen stand afar off (Psalm 38:11).

I became also a reproach unto them: when they looked upon me they shaked their heads (Psalm 109:25).

*Fulfillment*

And all his acquaintance, and the women that followed him from Galilee, stood afar off, beholding these things (Luke 23:49).

And they that passed by reviled him, wagging their heads (Matthew 27:39).

● The Messiah would be stared at and His crucifiers would cast lots for His garments:

*Prophecy*

I may tell all my bones: they look and stare upon me. They part my garments among them, and cast lots upon my vesture (Psalm 22:17,18).

*Fulfillment*

And the people stood beholding (Luke 23:35).

Then the soldiers, when they had crucified Jesus, took his garments, and made four parts . . . now the coat was without seam, woven from the top throughout. They said therefore among themselves, Let us not rend it, but cast lots for it, whose it shall be: that the scripture might be fulfilled, which saith, They parted my raiment among them, and for my vesture they did cast lots. These things therefore the soldiers did (John 19:23,24).

- The Messiah would suffer thirst, but would be given gall and vinegar to drink:

*Prophecy*

They gave me also gall for my meat; and in my thirst they gave me vinegar to drink (Psalm 69:21).

*Fulfillment*

After this, Jesus knowing that all things were now accomplished, that the scripture might be fulfilled, saith, I thirst. Now there was set a vessel full of vinegar, and they filled a sponge with vinegar, and put it upon hyssop, and put it to his mouth (John 19:28,29).

- The Messiah would cry out to God at death, and commit His spirit to Him:

*Prophecy*

My God, My God, why hast thou forsaken me? (Psalm 22:1).

Into thine hand I commit my spirit (Psalm 31:5).

*Fulfillment*

And about the ninth hour Jesus cried with a loud voice, saying, Eli, Eli lama sabachthani? that is to say, My God, my God, why hast thou forsaken me? (Matthew 27:46).

And when Jesus had cried with a loud voice, he said, Father, into thy hands I commend my spirit: and having said thus, he gave up the ghost (Luke 23:46).

- At the death of the Messiah there would be darkness over the land:

*Prophecy*

And it shall come to pass in that day, saith the Lord GOD, that I will cause the sun to go down at noon, and I will darken the earth in the clear day (Amos 8:9).

*Fulfillment*

Now from the sixth hour there was darkness over all

the land (Matthew 27:45).

● The Messiah would be buried in a rich man's tomb:

*Prophecy*

And he made his grave with the wicked, and with the rich in his death; because he had done no violence, neither was any deceit in his mouth (Isaiah 53:9).

*Fulfillment*

When the even was come, there came a rich man of Arimathæa, named Joseph, who also himself was Jesus' disciple: He went to Pilate, and begged the body of Jesus. Then Pilate commanded the body to be delivered. And when Joseph had taken the body, he wrapped it in a clean linen cloth, and laid it in his own new tomb, which he had hewn out in the rock: and he rolled a great stone to the door of the sepulchre, and departed (Matthew 27:57-60).

● The Messiah would be resurrected from the dead:

*Prophecy*

For thou wilt not leave my soul in hell; neither wilt thou suffer thine Holy One to see corruption (Psalm 16:10).

*Fulfillment*

He seeing this before spake of the resurrection of Christ, that his soul was not left in hell, neither his flesh did see corruption. This Jesus hath God raised up, whereof we all are witnesses (Acts 2:31,32).

● The Messiah would ascend on high, even to the right hand of God:

*Prophecy*

Thou hast ascended on high, thou hast led captivity captive; thou hast received gifts for men; yea, for the rebellious also, that the LORD God might dwell among them (Psalm 68:18).

The LORD said unto my Lord, Sit thou at my right hand, until I make thine enemies thy footstool (Psalm 110:1).

*Fulfillment*

And when he had spoken these things, while they beheld, he was taken up; and a cloud received him out of their sight (Acts 1:9).

. . . when he had by himself purged our sins, sat down on the right hand of the Majesty on high (Hebrews 1:3).

Behold, I see the heavens opened, and the Son of man standing on the right hand of God (Acts 7:56).

These are just a few of the prophecies from the Scriptures about the Messiah that have been fulfilled in Jesus of Nazareth. Other men came among the Jews, both before and after Jesus, proclaiming that they were the Messiah. In every case, regrettably, they fared better among the scribes and ministers than did Jesus. Yet none, not one, of the Old Testament prophecies was fulfilled in them, and all of their own prophecies utterly failed. The consequences of their actions brought terrible destructions upon the Jewish people.

## Daniel's Timetable

Probably one of the most startling prophecies of the coming Messiah is from the book of Daniel where the year of the Messiah's being killed is set forth. This prophet gives us the time frame in which the Messiah would be cut off from the land of the living:

Seventy weeks are determined upon thy people and upon thy holy city, to finish the transgression, and to make an end of sins, and to make reconciliation for iniquity, and to bring in everlasting righteousness, and to seal up the vision and prophecy, and to anoint the most Holy.

Know therefore and understand, that from the going forth of the commandment to restore and to build Jerusalem unto the Messiah the Prince shall be seven weeks, and threescore and two weeks: the street shall be built again, and the wall, even in troublous times.

And after threescore and two weeks shall Messiah be cut off, but not for himself: and the people of the prince that shall come shall destroy the city and the sanctuary; and the end thereof shall be with a flood, and unto the end of the war desolations are determined (Daniel 9:24-26).

In Hebrew the word for "week," *shabua,* means "seven," and could mean a week of seven days or seven years. We divide our week into seven days and our years usually into a decade or ten years. The Hebrews, on the other hand, recognized the periods of seven days and seven years as their "week" of days and years.

In the prophecy of Daniel, the prophet has reference not to seventy weeks of days, but of years (see Leviticus 25:8). To understand the prophecy, we must first understand a bit of the history behind it.

The prophets in Jerusalem, which included Jeremiah, Baruch and Obadiah, had warned the inhabitants of Judea and its capital Jerusalem to repent or they would be carried away by the Babylonians. This warning was rejected, and Nebuchadnezzar, with his armies, conquered and plundered Judea, taking most of the people captive into Babylon.

Daniel was one of the princes of Judea who was taken. Because he was a prophet chosen by God, Daniel could interpret the dreams of the Babylonian emperor Nebuchadnezzar, so he became Nebuchadnezzar's chief advisor. Daniel prayed fervently, beseeching the Lord to forgive him of his sins, and praying for the redemption of all Israel. One day, while at evening prayer, Daniel was visited by the angel Gabriel who told him that seventy weeks of years were determined to "make an end of sins, and to . . . anoint the most Holy" (Daniel 9:24). The angel said that from the commandment to restore Jerusalem to the coming of Prince Messiah would be 69 weeks of years. Furthermore, the angel declared that the Messiah would be killed, "cut off, but not for himself" (He was to die for others), and that afterward the city (Jerusalem) and the sanctuary (the Temple) would be destroyed. The Temple rites of the Jews would then cease, this being the abomination of desolation (Matthew 24:15).

We know that the first abomination of desolation occurred in A.D. 70 when the Romans destroyed Jerusalem and the Temple so utterly that not one stone was left upon another at the Temple site. Jesus had predicted this before His death and resurrection, in Matthew 24:2. The Jews have not had Temple worship since that time. Thus, according to what the angel Gabriel said, the Messiah must have come before A.D. 70.

Since Gabriel told Daniel just when the Messiah would come, let us see how this vision was fulfilled. The "commandment to restore and build Jerusalem" and the Temple is known in Holy Writ and history as the Decree of Artaxerxes.

In 445 B.C. a Jew named Nehemiah, who was the king's cupbearer, prayed unto God that the Lord might allow some of the Jews to return from the captivity to Jerusalem (then lying in ruins) to rebuild its walls and the Temple. The king learned of this request from his faithful servant, and he decreed that some of the Jews indeed were to return to Palestine to do that work. The decree was given on the first of Nisan in the 20th year of Artaxerxes, or March 14, 445 B.C. It took 49 years to rebuild the city; thus the seven weeks of years in verse 25 of Daniel 9.

The Messiah was to come at the end of 69 weeks of years. The Hebrews kept a lunar year of 360 days a year instead of our solar one with 365 1/4. By taking the 69 weeks times 7 years times 360 days we come to a total of 173,880 days. If we count 173,880 days from March 14, 445 B.C., we arrive at the date of April 6, 32 A.D..

According to our solar year it would be added a bit differently. From 445 B.C. to 32 A.D there are 476 years (1 B.C. to A.D. 1 is one year). By taking 476 years times 365 days we come to 173,740 days. When we add for leap years we come up with another 116 days. Then if we add the days from March 14 (1 Nisan) to April 6, we come to the same total of 173,880 days.

Thus, the angel Gabriel told Daniel that the Messiah would be cut off from the land of the living, but not for Himself—this would make reconciliation for sin—and it would occur on the 6th of April, A.D. 32. On this very day, Jesus of Nazareth died on the cross of Calvary just outside of Jerusalem.

# VII Choose You This Day

Today in the world there are perhaps in excess of four hundred different Aquarian "bibles," all claiming to be the Word of God. Yet there is today, as yesterday, only *one* Christian Bible, and it *is* the Word of God. The Aquarian bibles and the Christian Bible contradict each other on every belief and practice! Both cannot be right!

Many centuries ago the prophet Elijah and more than four hundred "prophets of Baal" (Lucifer) gathered upon Mt. Carmel for a contest. The people had been thinking they could worship the Lord while still believing the teachings and practicing the occultic arts that the prophets of Baal told them to.

We read in 1 Kings 18:21:

And Elijah came unto all the people, and said, How long halt ye between two opinions? If the LORD be God, follow him: but if Baal, then follow him.

Elijah put both the god of the prophets of Baal and his own God to a test. He told them to call upon their god to bring down fire to consume an offering, and he said he would do the same. The prophets of Baal cried, screamed, pleaded, and even cut themselves in order to get Baal to hear them, but nothing happened. Elijah then had the altar drenched three times with water. He called upon the

Lord in a simple prayer, and suddenly, fire came down from heaven! The fire not only consumed the offering, but it also consumed the wood, the stone altar and the water in the trenches surrounding the altar.

It is my prayer that in this book I have shown you the power of the Word of God, the Bible, versus the powerless deception of the modern "prophets of Baal" (who promote astrology, necromancy, reincarnation, etc.). I hope I have shown you that you cannot serve two masters. I hope you will be honest with yourself, and with God. You have a very important decision to make. This life will last but a brief moment, yet your eternal soul will exist forever.

Some of you may reject all the reasonable evidence and continue to believe in astrology, channeling and reincarnation. However, in doing so you now will be conscious of the fact that you are going against the Bible and the God whose Word it is. You need to claim the biblical Jesus as your own. It is my hope that you will choose life over death, and salvation over destruction.

After being raised a Theosophist (a member of the foremost Aquarian missionary society), and a dedicated Aquarian who sat at the feet of the New Age "John the Baptist," I became a Christian. I came to realize that the way of sin is death, but Jesus is the way to salvation!

## To the Aquarian

You are a person who wants peace and prosperity for all humanity. You want the world to be clean from pollution. You want the people of the world to be free from hunger and oppression. You are concerned about your eternal soul and the future of mankind. Be assured that God loves you, and He wants, just like you, what is best for humanity, His children.

Let me ask you a few questions:

1. Is astrology biblical, or even scientific?

2. Is reincarnation a biblical doctrine as Aquarian ministers preach?

3. Do channeled messages correspond with biblical messages?

4. Is psychic prophecy trustworthy?

After you have pondered and answered the above questions, please consider these:

1. Does the Mazzaroth testify of Jesus Christ?

2. What does it testify about Him?

3. How can you pay back your spiritual debt?

4. What does God, through the Bible, tell you to do?

If you were able to answer all of these questions, one way or the other, you are ready for a choice. The time is now. If you choose to follow Aquarianity, you know that you have rejected the God and Christ of the Bible.

If you choose to turn to Christianity, you must (1) recognize you are a sinner in need of salvation, and (2) confess with your mouth and believe in your heart that Jesus is the Lord of your life and your Redeemer. Ask Jesus into your heart today.

If you have chosen Christianity, the next step is to find a church that preaches the Word of God. There are many churches that claim to be Christian but are not. There are other so-called Christian churches which do not preach the Word of God. You must find a church that looks to the Bible for all of its beliefs and practices. Pray that God may direct you. He will—you are His now.

So, as the prophet Joshua urged so long ago,

Choose you this day whom ye will serve (Joshua 24:15).

As for me, and my house, we will serve the Lord Jesus.

# REFERENCE NOTES

## Chapter III – Astrology: Science or Superstition?

1. Gallup Poll, October 19, 1975, published in Sylvia Cranston and Carey Williams, *Reincarnation: A New Horizon in Science, Religion and Society* (New York: Julian Press, 1984), p. 12.

2. Geofrey Dean, "Does Astrology Need to Be True? Part One: A Look at the Real Thing," *The Skeptical Inquirer,* vol. 9, no. 2, pp. 113-14.

3. Ibid.

4. Ibid, p. 167.

5. Henry Weingarten, *A Modern Introduction to Astrology* (New York: ASI Publishers, 1974), p. 28.

6. John Godwin, *Occult America* (Garden City, NY: Doubleday & Co., 1972), p. 3.

7. William J. Petersen, *Those Curious New Cults* (New Canaan, CT: Keats Publications, 1973), p. 14.

8. Gary Keen in *Spiritual, Metaphysical and New Trends in Modern Astrology,* Joan McEvers, editor (St. Paul, MN: Llewellyn Publications, 1988), p. 17.

9. June Wakefield, *Cosmic Astrology: The Religion of the Stars* (Lakemont, GA: CSA Press, 1968), p. 11.

10. John Manolesco, *Scientific Astrology* (New York: Pinnacle Books, 1973), p. 2.

11. Michel Gauquelin, *The Cosmic Clocks,* (Chicago: Henry Regnery Co., 1976) p. 85.

12. Paul Carderc, L'Astrologie, "Que Sais – Je?" 508:3rd ed., Paris: Presses Universitaires De France, 1961, p. 89, quoted by John W. Montgomery, *Principalities and Powers: The World of the Occult* (Minneapolis, MN: Bethany House Publishers, 1976), pp. 105-6.

13. Gauquelin, *Cosmic Clocks,* p. 81.

14. *Human Behavior* (April 1975), p. 31.

15. Joseph F. Goodavage, *Astrology: The Space-Age Science* (New York: Signet, 1967), p. 15.

16. W. Keith Eriksen, "The Inaccuracy of Astrological Research," *The Humanist* (November/December 1976), pp. 43-44.

17. Ibid.

18. Michel Gauquelin, *The Scientific Basis of Astrology: Myth or Reality* (New York: Stein and Day, 1973).

19. Michel Gauquelin, *Dreams and Illusions of Astrology* (Buffalo, NY: Prometheus Books, 1979).

20. Michel Guaquelin, *Birth Times, A Scientific Investigation of the Secrets of Astrology* (New York: Hill & Wang, 1983), p. 139.

21. Guaquelin, *Scientific Basis of Astrology,* p. 145.

22. Robert Eisler, *The Royal Art of Astrology* (London: Herbert Joseph, 1946) p. 28.

23. *Time,* March 21, 1969, p. 56.

24. Ronald Davison, *Astrology* (New York: A.R.C. Books, 1963), p. 94.

25. Nicholas De Vore, *Encyclopedia of Astrology* (Totowa, NJ: Littlefield Adams & Co., 1976), p. 8.

26. Jeff Mayo, *Astrology* (London: Hodder & Stoughton Ltd., 1978), p. 7.

27. Arthur Dione, *Jungian Birth Charts: How to Interpret the Horoscope Using Jungian Psychology* (Wellington, North Amptonshire, England: The Aquarian Press, 1988), p. 83.

28. Alice O. Howell, *Jungian Symbolism in Astrology* (Wheaton, IL: Quest, 1987), p. 18.

29. Irene Diamond, *Astrology and the Holy Bible* (privately published, 1983), p. 162.

30. Alan Oken, *Astrology, Evolution and Revolution: A Path to Higher Consciousness Through Astrology* (New York: Bantam, 1976), p. 25.

31. J. B. Lightfoot, trans., *The Apostolic Fathers* (Grand Rapids, MI: Baker Book House, 1956), p. 12.

32. Merrill F. Unger, *Demons in the World Today* (Wheaton, IL: Tyndale House Publishers, 1971), p. 9.

33. E. Russell, *Astrology and Prediction* (New York: Drake Publications, 1973), p. 13.

34. Ibid.

35. R. Noorberger, *The Soul Hustlers,* (Grand Rapids, MI: Zondervan Publishing Company, 1976), p. 18.

36. James T. Braha, *Ancient Hindu Astrology for the Modern Western Astrologer* (North Miami, FL: Hermetician Press, 1986), p. 306.

37. Eisler, *Royal Art,* p. 21.

## Chapter IV – Reincarnation: The Wheel of Rebirth

1. *London Daily Telegraph,* April 15, 1979, quoted in Sylvia Cranston and Carey Williams, *Reincarnation: A New Horizon in Science, Religion and Society* (New York: Julian Press, 1984), p. 13.

2. George Gallup, Jr., *Adventures in Immortality* (New York: McGraw-Hill, 1982), pp. 137-38, 192-93.

3. *Journal of Nervous and Mental Disease* (September 1977), p. 172.

4. *Encyclopedia Britannica, Macropedia,* XVIII:276-78.

5. Helena P. Blavatsky, *The Secret Doctrine,* vol. 3 (Los Angeles: Theosophy Co., 1925), p. 386.

6. Ibid, p. 246.

7. Helena P. Blavatsky, *The Key to Theosophy* (Chicago: Theosophical Publishing House, 1930), p. 111.

8. Helena P. Blavatsky, *Collected Writings,* vol. 8 (Chicago: Theosophical Publishing House, 1930), p. 277.

9. Blavatsky, *Secret Doctrine,* vol. 3, p. 386.

10. Jane Roberts, *Seth Speaks: The Eternal Validity of the Soul* (Englewood Cliffs, NJ: Prentice-Hall Inc., 1972), p. 138.

11. Elizabeth Kubler-Ross, *Death: A Final Stage of Growth* (Englewood Cliffs, NJ: Prentice-Hall, 1975), p. 166.

12. Leslie Weatherhead, *The Christian Agnostic* (Nashville: Abingdon Press, 1972), p. 45.

13. Weatherhead, *Christian Agnostic,* p. 209.

14. Josephus, *Jewish Wars,* book II, chapter 8, paragraph 14.

15. Joseph P. Grudel, Robert M. Bowman, Jr., Dan Schlesinger, "Reincarnation – Did the Church Suppress It?" *Christian Research Journal,* vol. 10:1 (Summer 1987), p. 10.

16. Origen, *Commentary on Matthew,* XIII.1.

17. Benjamin Creme, "Reincarnation and Karma in the Bible," *Share International* (Special Information Issue, 1986), p. 19.

18. Ibid.

19. Ibid.

20. Ibid.

## Chapter V – Channeling: Is It From God?

1. William F. Barrett, "On Some Experiments With the Ouija Board and Blindfolded Sitters," *Proceedings of the American Society for Psychical Research* (September 1914), p. 394.

2. Nandor Fodor, *The Guide Book for the Study of Psychical Research* (New Hyde Park, NY: University Books, 1966), p 182.

3. Carl Wickland, M.D., psychiatrist quoted by Edmond C. Gruss in *Cults and the Occult in the Age of Aquarius* (Grand Rapids, MI: Baker Book House, 1974), p. 106.

4. Raupert J. Godfrey, "The Truth About the Ouija Board," *The Ecclesiastical Review* (November 1918), pp. 474-75.

5. H. R. Neff, *Psychic Phenomenon and Religion*, quoted by Edmond C. Gruss, *Cults and the Occult in the Age of Aquarius* (Grand Rapids, MI: Baker Book House, 1974), p. 131.

6. Jane Roberts, *Seth Speaks: The Eternal Validity of the Soul* (Englewood Cliffs, NJ: Prentice-Hall Inc., 1972), pp. 435-36.

7. Douglas J. Mahr, *Voyage to the New World* (Friday Harbor, WA: Masterworks, 1985), p. 228.

## Chapter VI – Prophecy: True or False?

1. James Bjornstad, *Twentieth Century Prophecy* (Minneapolis, MN: Dimension Books, 1969), pp. 29-36.

2. Ibid, pp. 38-44.

# Bibliography

Allen, Marcus. *Astrology for the New Age: An Intuitive Approach.* Sebastopol, CA: CRCS Publications, 1979.

Ankerberg, John and Weldon, John. *Astrology: Do the Heavens Rule Our Destiny?* Eugene, OR: Harvest House Publishers, 1989.

Barrett, William F. "On Some Experiments With the Ouija Board and Blindfolded Sitters." *Proceedings of the American Society for Psychical Research,* September 1914.

Bjornstad, James. *Twentieth Century Prophecy.* Minneapolis, MN: Dimension Books, 1969.

Blavatsky, Helena P. *Collected Writings.* Chicago, IL: Theosophical Publishing House, 1930.

____. *The Key to Theosophy.* Chicago: Theosophical Publishing House, 1930.

____. *The Secret Doctrine.* Los Angeles: Theosophy Co., 1925.

Braha, James T. *Ancient Hindu Astrology for the Modern Western Astrologer.* North Miami, FL: Hermetician Press, 1986.

Bullinger, E. W. *The Witness of the Stars.* Grand Rapids, MI: Kregel, 1967.

Creme, Benjamin. "Reincarnation and Karma in the Bible," *Share International,* Special Information Issue, 1986.

Davison, Ronald. *Astrology.* New York: A.R.C. Books, 1963.

____. *Synastry: Understanding Human Relations Through Astrology.* New York: ASI Publishers, 1978.

Dean, Geofrey. "Does Astrology Need to Be True? Part One: A Look at the Real Thing," *The Skeptical Inquirer,* vol. 9, no. 2.

De Vore, Nicholas. *Encyclopedia of Astrology.* Totowa, NJ: Littlefield Adams & Co., 1976.

Diamond, Irene. *Astrology and the Holy Bible.* Privately published, 1983.

Dione, Arthur. *Jungian Birth Charts: How to Interpret the Horoscope Using Jungian Psychology.* Wellington, North Amptonshire, England: The Aquarian Press, 1988.

Eisler, Robert. *The Royal Art of Astrology.* London: Herbert Joseph, Ltd., 1946.

Eriksen, W. Keith. "The Inaccuracy of Astrological Research," *The Humanist,* November/December 1976.

Fleming, Kenneth C. *God's Voice in the Stars: Zodiac Signs and Biblical Truth.* Neptune, NJ: Loizeauz Brothers, 1987.

Fodor, Nandor. *The Guide Book for the Study of Psychical Research.* New Hyde Park, NY: University Books, 1966.

Fox, Emmet. *The Zodiac and the Bible.* New York: Harper & Row, 1961.

Gauquelin, Michel. *Birth Times: A Scientific Investigation of the Secrets of Astrology.* New York: Hill & Wang, 1983.

____. *The Scientific Basis of Astrology: Myth or Reality.* New York: Stein and Day, 1973.

Godfrey, Raupert J. "The Truth About the Ouija Board," *The Ecclesiastical Review,* November 1918.

Godwin, John. *Occult America.* Garden City, NY: Doubleday & Co., 1972.

Goetz, William R. *Apocalypse Next.* Beaverlodge, Alberta: Horizon House Publishers, 1980.

Goodavage, Joseph F. *Astrology: The Space Age Science.* New York: Signet, 1967.

Grudel, Joseph P., et al. "Reincarnation — Did the Church Suppress It?" *Christian Research Journal,* vol. 10, no. 1, Summer 1987.

Gruss, Edmond C. *Cults and the Occult in the Age of Aquarius.* Grand Rapids, MI: Baker Book House, 1974.

Howell, Alice O. *Jungian Symbolism in Astrology.* Wheaton, IL: Quest, 1987.

Koch, Kurt. *Between Christ and Satan.* Grand Rapids, MI: Kregel, 1962.

Lightfoot, J. B., trans. *The Apostolic Fathers.* Grand Rapids, MI: Baker Book House, 1956.

Logan, Daniel. *The Reluctant Prophet.* New York: Doubleday & Co., 1968.

Mahr, Douglas J. *Voyage to the New World.* Friday Harbor, WA: Masterworks, 1985.

Manolesco, John. *Scientific Astrology.* New York: Pinnacle Books, 1973.

Mayo, Jeff. *Astrology.* London: Hodder & Stoughton Ltd., 1978.

McEvers, Joan, editor. *Spiritual, Metaphysical and New Trends in Modern Astrology.* St. Paul, MN: Llewellyn Publications, 1988.

Mechler, et al. "Response to the National Enquirer Astrology Study," *The Skeptical Inquirer,* vol. 5, no. 2.

Newall, Victor. *The Encyclopedia of Witchcraft and Magic.* New York: Dial Press, 1974.

Oken, Alan. *Evolution and Revolution: A Path to Higher Consciousness Through Astrology.* New York: Bantam, 1976.

Petersen, William J. *Those Curious New Cults.* New Canaan, CT: Keats Publications, 1973.

Roberts, Jane. *Seth Speaks: The Eternal Validity of the Soul.* Englewood Cliffs, NJ: Prentice-Hall Inc., 1972.

Russell, E. *Astrology and Prediction.* New York: Drake Publications, 1973.

Seiss, Joseph A. *The Gospel in the Stars.* Grand Rapids, MI: Kregel, 1978.

Unger, Merrill. *Demons in the World Today.* Wheaton, IL: Tyndale House Publishers, 1971.

Wakefield, June. *Cosmic Astrology: The Religion of the Stars.* Lakemont, GA: CSA Press, 1968.

Weatherhead, Leslie. *The Christian Agnostic.* Nashville, TN: Abingdon Press, 1972.

Womack, David A. *12 Signs, 12 Sons: Astrology in the Bible.* New York: Harper & Row, 1978.